The Wadsworth Themes in American Literature Series

1492–1820

THEME 4

Contested Nations in the Early Americas

Ralph Bauer
University of Maryland

Jay Parini
Middlebury College
General Editor

WADSWORTH
CENGAGE Learning™

Australia • Brazil • Japan • Korea • Mexico • Singapore • Spain • United Kingdom • United States

WADSWORTH
CENGAGE Learning

The Wadsworth Themes in American Literature Series, 1492-1820
Theme 4: Contested Nations in the Early Americas
Ralph Bauer, Jay Parini

Publisher, Humanities: *Michael Rosenberg*

Senior Development Editor: *Michell Phifer*

Assistant Editor: *Megan Garvey*

Editorial Assistant: *Rebekah Matthews*

Associate Development Project Manager: *Emily A. Ryan*

Executive Marketing Manager: *Mandee Eckersley*

Senior Marketing Communications Manager: *Stacey Purviance*

Senior Project Manager, Editorial Production: *Lianne Ames*

Senior Art Director: *Cate Rickard Barr*

Senior Print Buyer: *Mary Beth Hennebury*

Permissions Editor: *Margaret Chamberlain-Gaston*

Permissions Researcher: *Writers Research Group, LLC*

Production Service: *Kathy Smith*

Text Designer: *Frances Baca*

Photo Manager: *Don Schlotman*

Photo Researcher: *Bryan Rinnert*

Cover Designer: *Frances Baca*

Cover Image: *Library of Congress*

Compositor: *Graphic World, Inc.*

© 2009 Wadsworth Cengage Learning

ALL RIGHTS RESERVED. No part of this work covered by the copyright herein may be reproduced, transmitted, stored, or used in any form or by any means graphic, electronic, or mechanical, including but not limited to photocopying, recording, scanning, digitizing, taping, Web distribution, information networks, or information storage and retrieval systems, except as permitted under Section 107 or 108 of the 1976 United States Copyright Act, without the prior written permission of the publisher.

For product information and technology assistance, contact us at
Cengage Learning Academic Resource Center, 1-800-423-0563
For permission to use material from this text or product,
submit all requests online at **www.cengage.com/permissions**.
Further permissions questions can be e-mailed to
permissionrequest@cengage.com.

Library of Congress Control Number: 2008925312

ISBN-13: 978-14282-6255-3

ISBN-10: 1-4282-6255-5

Wadsworth Cengage Learning
25 Thomson Place
Boston, 02210
USA

Cengage Learning products are represented in Canada by Nelson Education, Ltd.

For your course and learning solutions, visit
academic.cengage.com.

Purchase any of our products at your local college store or at our preferred online store **www.ichapters.com**.

We have made every effort to trace the ownership of all copyrighted material and to secure permission from copyright holders. In the event of any question arising as to the use of any material, we will be pleased to make the necessary corrections in future printings.

Printed in the United States of America
1 2 3 4 5 6 7 12 11 10 09 08

Contents

Prince Hall (ca. 1735–1807)   4
  To the Honorable Counsel & House of Representatives for the State
  of Massachusetts Bay in General Court assembled, January 13, 1777   5

Judith Sargent Murray (1751–1820)   6
  On the Equality of the Sexes   7

Phillis Wheatley (ca. 1753–1784)   15
  "On being brought from A F R I C A to A M E R I CA."   16
  "On Recollection"   17
  A Farewell to America. To Mrs. S. W.   18
  To His Excellency George Washington   20
  Letter to Reverend Samson Occum   21

Jupiter Hammon (1711–ca. 1806)   22
  An Address to Miss Phillis Wheatly [sic]   22

François Dominique Toussaint L'Ouverture (ca. 1743–1803)   25
  From The Memoir   26

Simón Bolívar (1783–1830)   30
  From The Jamaica Letter   31

Andrés Bello (1781–1865)   46
  Agriculture in the Torrid Zone   46

José María Heredia (1803–1839)   48
  Ode to Niagara   49

Juan Francisco Manzano (1797–1854)   52
  From The Autobiography of a Cuban Slave   53

Preface

WHAT IS AMERICA? HOW HAVE WE DEFINED OURSELVES over the past five centuries, and dealt with the conflict of cultures, the clash of nations, races, ethnicities, religious visions, and class interests? How have we thought about ourselves, as men and women, in terms of class and gender? How have we managed to process a range of complex and compelling issues?

The Wadsworth Themes in American Literature Series addresses these questions in a sequence of 21 booklets designed especially for classroom use in a broad range of courses. There is nothing else like them on the market. Each booklet has been carefully edited to frame issues of importance, with attention to the development of key themes. Teachers and students have consistently found these mini-anthologies immensely productive in the classroom, as the texts we have chosen are provocative, interesting to read, and central to the era under discussion. Each thematic booklet begins with a short essay that provides the necessary historical and literary context to address the issues raised in that theme. In addition, many of the headnotes have been written by scholars, with an eye to introducing students to the life and times of the author under discussion, paying attention to historical context as well, and making sure to prepare the way for the selection that follows. The footnotes provide useful glosses on words and phrases, keying the reader to certain historical moments or ideas, explaining oddities, offering extra material to make the texts more accessible.

Each of these themes is drawn from *The Wadsworth Anthology of American Literature,* which is scheduled for later publication. The first sequence of booklets, edited by Ralph Bauer at the University of Maryland, takes in the colonial period, which runs from the arrival of Columbus in the New World through 1820, a period of immense fluidity and dynamic cultural exchange. Bauer is a pioneering scholar who takes a hemispheric approach to the era, looking at the crush of cultures—Spanish, English, Dutch, German, French; each of these European powers sent colonial missions across the Atlantic Ocean, and the collision of these cultures with each other and with the Native American population (itself diverse and complicated) was combustive. Bauer isolates several themes, one of which is called "Between Cultures," and looks at the confrontation of European and Native American traditions. In "Spirituality, Church, and State in Colonial America," he examines the obsession with religious ideas, some of which led to the crisis in Salem, where the infamous witch trials occurred. In "Empire,

Science, and the Economy in the Americas," the focus shifts to the material basis for culture, and how it affected some outlying regions, such as Barbados, Peru, Mexico, and Alaska—thus blasting apart the rigid ways that scholars have more traditionally thought about North America in isolation. In "Contested Nations in the Early Americas," Bauer centers on revolutionary fervor in places like Haiti, Cuba, and Jamaica, where various groups fought for control of both territory and cultural influence.

In the second sequence of booklets, Shirley Samuels (who chairs the English Department at Cornell and has established herself as a major voice in the field of nineteenth-century American literature) looks at the early days of the American republic, a period stretching from 1800 to 1865, taking us through the Civil War. This was, of course, a period of huge expansion as well as consolidation. Manifest Destiny was a catchword, as the original thirteen colonies expanded in what Robert Frost referred to as "a nation gradually realizing westward." The question of identity arose on different fronts, and we see the beginnings of the women's movement here. In her first theme, Samuels looks at "The Woman Question," offering a selection of texts by men and women thinking about the place of a woman in society and in the home. Some of this writing is quite provocative, and much of it is rarely studied in college classrooms.

The racial questions came into focus during this era, too, and the groundwork for the Civil War was unhappily laid. In "Confronting Race," Samuels offers a searing medley of texts from Black Hawk through Frances E. W. Harper. These works hurl this topic into stark relief against a cultural landscape in perpetual ferment. This booklet includes selections from the speeches of Sojourner Truth, the pseudonym of an astonishing black woman, a former slave who became a leading abolitionist and advocate for women's rights.

In "Manifest Destiny and the Quest for the West," Samuels offers a mix of classic and lesser known texts on the theme of westward expansion, beginning with the remarkable *Journals of Lewis and Clark*, a key document in the literature of westward expansion and a vivid example of the literature of exploration. She ends with "Views of War," presenting a range of inspiring and heart-rending texts from a time of bloodshed, hatred, and immense idealism. The Union was very nearly broken, and one gets a full sense of the dynamics of this troubled era by comparing these texts by an unusual range of authors from Oliver Wendell Holmes and Julia Ward Howe through Sidney Lanier, one of the finest (if lesser known) poets of the era.

In the third sequence of booklets, Alfred Bendixen, who teaches at Texas A&M University, offers a selection from the period just after the Civil War through the beginnings of the modern period. Bendixen, who presides over the American Literature Association, has proven himself a scholar of unusual talents, and he brings his deep knowledge of the period into play here. In "Imagining Gender," he takes up where Samuels left off, looking at a compelling range of texts by men and women who consider the evolving issue of gender in fascinating ways. One sees the coalescing of the women's movement in some of this work, and also the resistance that inevitably arose, as women tried to assert themselves and to find their voice.

In "Questions of Social and Economic Justice," Bendixen puts forward texts by a range of key figures, including George Washington Cable, Hamlin Garland, Mary Wilkins Freeman, and Jack London. Each of these gifted writers meditates on the struggle of a young nation to define itself, to locate its economic pulse, to balance the need for economic expansion and development with the requirements and demands of social justice. Many of these themes carry forward into the twentieth century, and it is worth looking closely at the origins of these themes in an era of compulsive growth. Needless to say, this was also a period when millions of immigrants arrived from Southern and Eastern Europe, radically changing the complexion of the nation. Bendixen offers a unique blend of texts on the conflicts and questions that naturally followed the so-called Great Migration in "Immigration, Ethnicity, and Race." This section includes excerpts from Jane Addams's remarkable memoir of her time at Hull-House, a mansion in Chicago where she and her coworkers offered a range of social assistance and cultural programs to working class immigrants.

The most unusual theme in this sequence of booklets by Bendixen is "Crime, Mystery, and Detection." Here the student will find an array of gripping stories by some of the original authors in a field that forms the basis for contemporary popular fiction around the world. American readers in this period loved detective stories, and readers still do. The mix is quite unusual, and it remains fascinating to see how the genre found its legs and began to run, through a time when readers wished to apply all the tools of intelligence to their world, discovering its ways and meaning, trying to figure out "who done it" in so many ways.

Martha J. Cutter—a scholar of considerable range and achievement who now teaches at the University of Connecticut—edits the sequence of booklets dealing with the modern era, 1910–1945, a period of huge importance in American history and culture. The American empire came into its own in this era, recognized its muscles, and began to flex them—in ways productive and (at times) destructive. Cutter begins by looking at the women's movement, and how men reacted to certain inevitable pressures. In "The Making of the New Woman and the New Man," she charts the struggle between the sexes in a compelling range of texts, including works by Sui Sin Far, Edwin Arlington Robinson, James Weldon Johnson, Willa Cather, and John Steinbeck, among others. Of course, the subject of class had a massive impact on how people viewed themselves, and in "Modernism and the Literary Left," she presents a selection of works that deal with issues of class, money, and power. At the center of this sequence lies "May Day," one of F. Scott Fitzgerald's most luminous and provocative stories.

The New Negro Renaissance occurred during this period, a revival and consolidation of writing in a variety of genres by African Americans. Here Cutter offers a brilliant selection of key texts from this movement, including work by Langston Hughes and Zora Neale Hurston in "Racism and Activism." This booklet extends well beyond the Harlem Renaissance itself to work by Richard Wright, a major voice in African American literature.

As it must, the theme of war occupies a central place in one thematic booklet. In the first half of the twentieth century, world wars destroyed the lives of millions. Never had the world seen killing like this, or inhumanity and cruelty on a scale that beggars the imagination. The violence of these conflicts, and the cultural implications of such destruction, necessarily held the attention of major writers. And so, in "Poetry and Fiction of War and Social Conflict," we find a range of compelling work by such writers as Ezra Pound, H.D. (Hilda Doolittle), T. S. Eliot, and Edna St. Vincent Millay.

Henry Hart is a contemporary poet, biographer, and critic with a broad range of work to his credit (he holds a chair in literature at William and Mary College). His themes are drawn from the postwar era, and he puts before readers a seductive range of work by poets, fiction writers, and essayists. Many of the themes from earlier volumes continue here. For instance, Hart begins with "Race and Ethnicity in the Melting Pot," offering students a chance to think hard about the matter of ethnicity and race in contemporary America. With texts by James Baldwin and Malcolm X through Amy Tan and Ana Menéndez, he presents viewpoints that will prove challenging and provocative—perfect vehicles for classroom discussion.

In "Class Conflicts and the American Dream," Hart explores unstable, challenging terrain in a sequence of texts by major postwar authors from Martin Luther King, Jr. through Flannery O'Connor. Some of these works are extremely well known, such as John Updike's story, "A & P." Others, such as James Merrill's "The Broken Home" may be less familiar. This booklet, as a whole, provides a rich field of texts, and will stimulate discussion on many levels about the role of class in American society.

Similarly, Hart puts forward texts that deal with gender and sexuality in "Exploring Gender and Sexual Norms." From Sylvia Plath's wildly destructive poem about her father, "Daddy," through the anguished meditations in poetry of Adrienne Rich, Anne Sexton, Allen Ginsberg, and Frank O'Hara (among others), the complexities of sexuality and relationships emerge. In Gore Vidal's witty and ferocious look at homosexuality and anti-Semitism in "Pink Triangle and Yellow Star," students have an opportunity to think hard about things that are rarely put forward in frank terms. Further meditations on masculinity and as well as gay and lesbian sexualities occur in work by Pat Califia, Robert Bly, and Mark Doty. The section called "Witnessing War" offers some remarkable poems and stories by such writers as Robert Lowell, James Dickey, and Tim O'Brien—each of them writing from a powerful personal experience. In a medley of texts on "Religion and Spirituality," Hart explores connections to the sacred, drawing on work by such writers as Flannery O'Connor, Charles Wright, and Annie Dillard. As in earlier booklets, these thematic arrangements by Hart will challenge, entertain, and instruct.

In sum, we believe these booklets will stimulate conversations in class that should be productive as well as memorable, for teacher and student alike. The texts have been chosen because of their inherent interest and readability, and—in a sense—for the multiple ways in which they "talk" to each other. Culture is, of course, nothing more than good conversation, its elevation to a level of discourse. We, the editors of these thematic booklets, believe that the attractive arrangements of compelling texts will make a lasting impression, and will help to answer the question posed at the outset: What is America?

ACKNOWLEDGMENTS

We would like to thank the following readers and scholars who helped us shape this series: Brian Adler, Valdosta State University; John Alberti, Northern Kentucky University; Lee Alexander, College of William and Mary; Althea Allard, Community College of Rhode Island; Jonathan Barron, University of Southern Mississippi; Laura Behling, Gustavus Adolphus College; Peter Bellis, University of Alabama at Birmingham; Alan Belsches, Troy University Dothan Campus; Renee Bergland, Simmons College; Roy Bird, University of Alaska Fairbanks; Michael Borgstrom, San Diego State University; Patricia Bostian, Central Peidmont Community College; Jessica Bozek, Boston University; Lenore Brady, Arizona State University; Maria Brandt, Monroe Community College; Martin Buinicki, Valparaiso University; Stuart Burrows, Brown University; Shawrence Campbell, Stetson University; Steven Canaday, Anne Arundel Community College; Carole Chapman, Ivy Tech Community College of Indiana; Cheng Lok Chua, California State University; Philip Clark, McLean High School; Matt Cohen, Duke University; Patrick Collins, Austin Community College; Paul Cook, Arizona State University; Dean Cooledge, University of Maryland Eastern Shore; Howard Cox, Angelina College; Laura Cruse, Northwest Iowa Community College; Ed Dauterich, Kent State University; Janet Dean, Bryant University; Rebecca Devers, University of Connecticut; Joseph Dewey, University of Pittsburgh–Johnstown; Christopher Diller, Berry College; Elizabeth Donely, Clark College; Stacey Donohue, Central Oregon Community College; Douglas Dowland, The University of Iowa; Jacqueline Doyle, California State University, East Bay; Robert Dunne, Central Connecticut State University; Jim Egan, Brown University; Marcus Embry, University of Northern Colorado; Nikolai Endres, Western Kentucky University; Terry Engebretsen, Idaho State University; Jean Filetti, Christopher Newport University; Gabrielle Foreman, Occidental College; Luisa Forrest, El Centro College; Elizabeth Freeman, University of California–Davis; Stephanie Freuler, Valencia Community College; Andrea Frisch, University of Maryland; Joseph Fruscione, Georgetown University; Lisa Giles, University of Southern Maine; Charles Gongre, Lamar State College–Port Arthur;

Gary Grieve-Carlson, Lebanon Valley College; Judy Harris, Tomball College; Brian Henry, University of Richmond; Allan Hikida, Seattle Central Community College; Lynn Houston, California State University, Chico; Coleman Hutchison, University of Texas–Austin; Andrew Jewell, University of Nebraska–Lincoln; Marion Kane, Lake-Sumter Community College; Laura Knight, Mercer County Community College; Delia Konzett, University of New Hampshire; Jon Little, Alverno College; Chris Lukasik, Purdue University; Martha B. Macdonald, York Technical College; Angie Macri, Pulaski Technical College; John Marsh, University of Illinois at Urbana Champaign; Christopher T. McDermot, University of Alabama; Jim McWilliams, Dickinson State University; Joe Mills, North Carolina School of the Arts; Bryan Moore, Arkansas State University; James Nagel, University of Georgia; Wade Newhouse, Peace College; Keith Newlin, University of North Carolina Wilmington; Andrew Newman, Stony Brook University; Brian Norman, Idaho State University; Scott Orme, Spokane Community College; Chris Phillips, Lafayette College; Jessica Rabin, Anne Arundel Community College; Audrey Raden, Hunter College; Catherine Rainwater, St. Edward's University; Rick Randolph, Kaua; Joan Reeves, Northeast Alabama Community College; Paul Reich, Rollins College; Yelizaveta Renfro, University of Nebraska–Lincoln; Roman Santillan, College of Staten Island; Marc Schuster, Montgomery County Community College; Carol Singley, Rutgers–Camden; Brenda Siragusa, Corinthian Colleges Inc.; John Staunton, University of North Caroline–Charlotte; Ryan Stryffeler, Ivy Tech Community College of Indiana; Robert Sturr, Kent State University, Stark Campus; James Tanner, University of North Texas; Alisa Thomas, Toccoa Falls College; Nathan Tipton, The University of Memphis; Gary Totten, North Dakota State University; Tony Trigilio, Columbia College, Chicago; Pat Tyrer, West Texas A&M University; Becky Villarreal, Austin Community College; Edward Walkiewicz, Oklahoma State University; Jay Watson, University of Mississippi; Karen Weekes, Penn State Abington; Bruce Weiner, St. Lawrence University; Cindy Weinstein, California Institute of Technology; Stephanie Wells, Orange Coast College; Robert West, Mississippi State University; Diane Whitley Bogard, Austin Community College–Eastview Campus; Edlie Wong, Rutgers; and Beth Younger, Drake University.

In addition, we would like to thank the indefatigable staff at Cengage Learning/Wadsworth for their tireless efforts to make these booklets and the upcoming anthology a reality: Michael Rosenberg, Publisher; Michell Phifer, Senior Development Editor, Lianne Ames, Senior Content Project Manager, Megan Garvey, Assistant Editor; Rebekah Matthews, Editorial Assistant, Emily Ryan, Associate Development Project Manager, Mandee Eckersley, Managing Marketing Manager, Stacey Purviance, Marketing Communications Manager, and Cate Barr, Art Director. We would also like to thank Kathy Smith, Project Manager, for her patience and attention to detail.

—Jay Parini, Middlebury College

Contested Nations in the Early Americas

The United States in the Western Hemisphere

While the American Revolution had resulted in the political independence of the thirteen colonies from Great Britain and, later, in the founding of the United States, the event had in itself not fundamentally transformed society or changed the lives of the majority of its citizens. Statistically, income, wealth, and actual political representation were as inequitably distributed in the United States in 1800 as they had been at the end of British colonial rule in 1776, while slavery would remain intact for another sixty-five years. Yet, although the *event* of the American Revolution had not effected major socio-economic or socio-political changes, it was "radical" for the revolutionary *process* that it had set in motion, providing the logic, ethos, and rhetoric for virtually all expansions of citizenship and civil rights up to the present. The challenge to the colonial socio-political status quo that independence from Britain had left untouched began to emerge as early as the Revolutionary War, the years of confederacy, and the early Republic, when women, African Americans, and unpropertied whites strategically employed the language and principles of the Declaration of Independence to empower themselves within the new national order. Hence, such African Americans as Prince Hall, Phillis Wheatley, and Jupiter Hammon began to draw attention (though, necessarily, in often subtle ways) to the contradictions between the American emancipatory rhetoric and the perpetuation of slavery. At the same time, such women as Judith Sargent Murray began to demand political rights for women, who had neither political representation nor, in fact, any legal existence except as a wife, mother, or daughter of a man.

The struggle between those who wished to expand the principles of the American Revolution to include all of the people living in the new nation and those who wished to maintain the social status quo as it existed at the end of colonial times did not take place in the national vacuum of the United States. Rather, it encompassed the international context of a broader challenge to aristocratic power in Europe, the disintegration of European empires in the New World, and the abolition of the institution of slavery in much of the Western hemisphere well in advance of the United States. Thus, the French Revolution (1789), which was in part inspired by the American Revolution and drew its basic ideas from the same Enlightenment principles, initially invigorated many of the social progressives in America. However, the Revolution that had begun on the Enlightened principles of equality, liberty, and fraternity turned into what was widely perceived as a "Reign of Terror," as hundreds of members of the old aristocracy were put to the guillotine (including the monarchs).

This became a powerful cautionary tale in the rhetoric of social conservatives (such as Edmund Burke), who warned against the excesses that would result from giving too much power to the "mob." Furthermore, the French terror of "mob rule" sent shock waves through the United States, and especially the American South, when, in August 1791, a massive slave uprising erupted in the French colony Saint-Domingue, now known as Haiti, the first free nation to be created by former African slaves in 1804. The leaders of the revolt, most notably, François-Dominique Toussaint L'Ouverture, invoked the principles of the French Revolution in order to justify the overthrow of the colonial slave regime, which resulted in the creation of the second independent nation state in the Western hemisphere (after the United States). In the United States, the international developments in France and Haiti contributed to the rise of a reactionary conservatism that prevailed through the last decade of the eighteenth century, until the so-called "Jeffersonian Revolution of 1800" signaled a change toward a more democratic conception of citizenship—at least as far as white males were concerned—as Western territories were opened up for white settlement. Similarly, in Spanish America, where the white population remained a privileged minority in many parts of colonial society, the Haitian example was viewed with considerable unease and Spanish rule as the best safeguard against indigenous revolts. Indeed, in the 1780s, Peru had experienced numerous devastating Indian rebellions under the leadership of self-styled heirs of the ancient Inca dynasts, such as Juan Santos Atahualpa and José Gabriel Condorcanqui Tupac Amaru II, who, had they been successful, would have expelled from Peru not only Peninsular Spanish imperialists but also (and especially) the hated Euro-American settlers. Hence, in Latin America, the movements toward independence only commenced in the 1810s, after Spain had herself been invaded by Napoleon and Spanish imperial power had effectively collapsed. Indigenous resistance to the Euro-American nation state continues to this day in many parts of Latin America.

Throughout the hemisphere, the American nation states were established on violently expropriated Indian lands. Many Native Americans were painfully aware that white Americans' independence spelled disaster for America's Native peoples. It is therefore no coincidence that many Native tribes had sided with the British Empire, not with the American revolutionaries, in the War of Independence—for which they were later punished by vengeful settlers. Insofar as the success of Jeffersonian egalitarianism depended on westward expansion, white Americans' "freedom" from the social hierarchies of the Old World was purchased with the genocide perpetrated against Native Americans during the nineteenth century. Nor did the rise of Jeffersonian democracy in the United States initially benefit Black slaves. On the contrary, the early decades of the nineteenth century witnessed the articulation of a coherent ideology of white male national citizenship predicated on a scientific racism that attempted to prove the biological existence and superiority of a "white race" of human beings. In addition to a restrictive concept of citizenship, doctrines of "manifest destiny" emerged that held that this white American male alone was destined by the laws of nature to inherit the American continent.

The rise of this racist conception of nationhood and history, as well as the persistence of slavery, drove the United States into an early isolationism, and even aggressive imperialism, vis-à-vis the other American nation states that were newly forming in the hemisphere. Thus, in 1826, when Simón Bolívar, the "George Washington of Latin America," summoned representatives from all the newly independent American nations of the Western hemisphere to a pan-American congress in Panama—called the Amphictyonic Congress, after the Amphictyonic League of Ancient Greece—in order to create a league of American republics with a common military, a mutual defense pact, and a supranational parliamentary assembly, the United States remained absent. While some U.S. officials, most notably President John Quincy Adams and Secretary of State Henry Clay, had wanted the United States to attend, politicians from the Southern states held up the mission by not approving funds or confirming the U.S. delegates because they knew that much of Latin America had outlawed slavery and that the abolition of slavery throughout the hemisphere would inevitably be on the Congress's agenda. They insisted that slavery was strictly a domestic affair and that international involvement on the issue amounted to an encroachment on America's independence and "freedom." Congress did, finally, approve two delegates to be sent. One of them, Richard C. Anderson, died en route to Panama, while the other, John Sergeant, arrived there only after the Congress was over.

Thus, in the United States, the issue of slavery would remain unresolved until the cataclysmic Civil War. The only other two places in the Western hemisphere where slavery was still being practiced by 1830 were Cuba and Brazil, both still under colonial rule. However, internationally, abolitionist sentiments rapidly gathered strength. One of the most fascinating literary documents to be produced by this international abolitionist movement was the autobiography of Juan Francisco Manzano, a Cuban slave and poet who had been encouraged to write by a circle gathering around the Cuban patriot Domingo del Monte. Manzano's autobiography was first published in English translation by the English abolitionist Richard Madden in London.

The United States and the "Disunited States"

The absence of the United States at the Congress of Panama may, in the end, have been inconsequential, as the grand league of American states envisioned by Bolívar remained a dream, and even his "Gran Colombia," an early South American state emerging from Spanish American independence, soon disintegrated into four separate nations—Colombia, Ecuador, Panama, and Venezuela—to join the rest of the modern "disunited states" of Latin America. Moreover, although slavery was abolished in all of these new Latin American nation states, they similarly failed to implement a social and political system in which wealth and political power were substantially more equitably distributed across various social groups than they had been during colonial times. Not unlike in the U.S. American South after the Civil War, in postcolonial Latin America, the estates that the Euro-American elites had established on Native American land with unfree labor were left largely untouched, as the old neo-feudal *encomiendas* (or grants of Indian tribute labor) of colonial times were transformed into enormous private landholdings (*haciendas*), on which an impoverished rural (and mainly Indian) proletariat was forced to work by economic necessity. Yet, ironically, as in Anglo America during the War of Independence, in Revolutionary Spanish America white and mestizo (or racially mixed) nationalists had frequently invoked the symbols of the Native American past in their efforts to define a national identity that was independent from Spain and even appealed to the Indians with promises of freedom and equality that independence would bring. Thus, in the 1820s, Bolívar had the ancient Inca temple of Pachacamac reconstructed (it had lain in ruins since the European conquest), while San Martín, a mestizo revolutionary addressing the Araucanians of Argentina in 1816, proclaimed that "I am an Indian too" in order to mobilize the Indian sectors for his campaign for independence. Despite all the historical evidence to the contrary, Spanish American nationalists, like some of their Anglo American counterparts, fancied their newly independent nation states as the fulfillment of the Native American past after several centuries of European imperial interregnum. Also not unlike some of their U.S. American counterparts, Spanish American literary nationalists such as Andrés Bello and José Maria Heredia invoked the symbols of the Western hemisphere's unique landscapes and natural beauties in their attempt to articulate an authentic American cultural identity and literary expression.

Prince Hall   ca. 1735–1807

A prominent leader of Boston's black community in the late eighteenth century, Prince Hall is perhaps most notable for founding the world's first lodge of black Freemasons. We have little factual information about his family and early life. Born sometime between 1735 and 1738 at a place still unknown, by 1749 he was working as an urban slave for a Boston leather dresser, William Hall. From the year 1762, he was a member of the Reverend Andrew Crosswell's Congregational church and married at age twenty-seven. In 1770, he received his manumission from William Hall and continued to work as an independent leather dresser and perhaps as a shop owner. On March 6, 1775, just before the commencement of armed conflict in the Revolutionary War, Hall and fourteen other black men became members of a lodge of Free and Accepted Masons, Army Lodge No. 441, attached to a British regiment composed primarily of Irish volunteers stationed in Boston. A few weeks later, Hall petitioned Joseph Warren and John Hancock, both American Masons, to allow free and enslaved blacks to enlist in Revolutionary militias. Although this petition was initially rejected, General Washington later reconsidered and permitted free blacks to serve, and Hall himself most likely fought in the War. From 1777 onward, Prince Hall was active expanding black membership in the Masons and lobbying for African Americans in general. He established new lodges in New York, Philadelphia, and Baltimore, and wrote numerous letters to London Masonic officials, the Countess of Huntingdon, Boston newspapers, as well as prominent blacks in Providence and Philadelphia. Most importantly, in 1777, he solicited the abolition of slavery in

Massachusetts and, in 1787, he petitioned (albeit unsuccessfully) for the public education for children of taxpaying Boston blacks. The same year, Hall, with 73 other blacks, also petitioned the General Court for financial or other assistance in support of plans for blacks to emigrate for Africa. Until his death in 1807, Hall continued to function as a leader in the promotion of the rights of black people, hosting prominent black ministers such as John Marrant, petitioning successfully for the release of black Boston residents who were kidnapped into slavery, and protesting discriminatory laws and practices.

Further Reading Sidney Kaplan, "Prince Hall: Organizer," in *The Black Presence in the Era of the American Revolution, 1770–1800* (1989 [1973]); Maurice Wallace, "'Are We Men?' Prince Hall, Martin Delany, and the Masculine Ideal in Black Freemasonry, 1775–1865," *American Literary History* 9.3 (Fall 1997): 396–424; Charles Wesley, *Prince Hall: Life and Legacy* (1977).

To the Honorable Counsel & House of Representatives for the State of Massachusetts Bay in General Court assembled, January 13, 1777[†]

THE PETITION OF A GREAT NUMBER OF BLACKS DETAINED IN A STATE OF SLAVERY IN THE BOWELS OF A FREE & CHRISTIAN COUNTY HUMBLY SHOWING

that your petitioners apprehend that they have in common with all other men a natural and unalienable right to that freedom which the great parent of the universe that hath bestowed equally on all mankind, & which they have never forfeited by any compact or agreement whatever—But that where unjustly dragged by the hand of cruel power, from their dearest friends & some of them even torn from the embraces of their tender parents. From a populous, pleasant and plentiful country and in violation of Laws of Nature and of Nations and in Defiance of all the tender feelings of humanity Brought here Either to Be sold like Beast of burthen & Like them Condemned to Slavery for Life. Among a People Professing the mild Religion of Jesus A people Not Insensible of the Secrets of Rational Being Nor without spirit to Resent the unjust endeavors of others to Reduce them to a state of Bondage and Subjugation your honour Need not to be informed that A Live of Slavery Like that of your petitioners Deprived of Every social privilege of Every thing Requisite and render Life Tolable is far worse that Nonexistance.

(In imitat)ion of the Lawdable Example of the Good People of these States your petitioners have Long and Patiently waited the Event of petition after petition. By them presented to the Legislative Body of this state[1] and cannot but with Grief Reflect that

---

[†] Source: Prince Hall, *To the Honorable Counsel & House of Representatives for the State of Massachusetts Bay in General Court assembled, January 13, 1777* (Boston, 1788).

[1] **this state:** Massachusetts; slaves there had submitted a series of petitions earlier in the 1770s.

their Success hath been but too similar they Cannot but express their Astonishment that It have Never Bin Considered that Every Principle from which America has Acted in the Course of their unhappy Difficulties with Great Briton Pleads Stronger than A thousand arguments in favors of your petitioners they therefore humble Beseech your honours to give this petition its due weight and consideration & cause an act of the legislature to be past Wherby they may be Restored to the Enjoyments of that which is the Natural right of all men and their Children who were Born in this Land of Liberty may not be held as Slaves after they arrive at the age of twenty-one years; so may the Inhabitance of this State No longer be chargeable with the inconstancy of acting themselves that part which they condemn and oppose in others, Be prospered in their present Glorious struggle for Liberty, and have those Blessings to them, &c.

—1788

Judith Sargent Murray 1751–1820

A gifted poet, editor, and playwright, Judith Sargent Murray was the eldest child of Captain Winthrop Sargent and Judith Saunders, a prominent merchant family in Gloucester, Massachusetts. As she showed notable intellectual promise as a child, her parents allowed her to study Greek and Latin along with her brother, Winthrop, who was studying at Harvard to become a minister. Nevertheless, Murray always regretted the fact that, as a woman, she was denied a formal education and therefore dedicated herself to women's education. At eighteen she married Captain John Stevens, a prosperous ship captain and merchant, but the marriage does not appear to have been a very happy one. When Stevens lost his ships and cargo during the Revolution, he fled the country in 1786 and died that same year on the island of St. Eustatius. Meanwhile, Judith had begun to publish her poems in 1784, contributing pieces to Boston magazines. She was remarried in 1788 to John Murray, a Universalist minister who had been a long-time family friend. The couple shared both spiritual and intellectual interests, and Reverend Murray encouraged his wife's literary efforts. After the couple moved to Boston, Murray was exposed to broader intellectual circles, and her poetry was published frequently in the *Massachusetts Magazine*. A series of Murray's magazine essays collectively entitled "The Gleaner," which formed a narrative about the life of a fictitious woman and addressed questions of equality in education and opportunities for women, appeared under the pseudonym "Constantia" from 1792 to 1794. During this time, she also wrote several plays, including *The Medium; or, The Happy Tea-Party* and *The Traveller Returned,* for the newly reopened Federal Street Theatre. With the help of friends and supporters, Murray undertook the production of a collected work of her poetry, plays, and essays, which appeared in three volumes as *The Gleaner. A Miscellaneous Production* in 1798. Also, Murray worked with her husband on editing his letters and papers for publication, and she published his autobiography in 1816 under the title *Records of the Life of John Murray*—one year after his death. She died in Natchez, Mississippi, in 1820, at the home of her surviving daughter, Julia.

Further Reading Sheila Skemp, *Judith Sargent Murray: A Brief Biography with Documents* (1998); Kirstin Wilcox, "The Scribblings of a Plain Man and the Temerity of a Woman: Gender and Genre in Judith Sargent Murray's *The Gleaner,*" *Early American Literature* 30.2 (1995): 121–144.

From On the Equality of the Sexes[†]

Gentlemen,

The following *ESSAY* is yielded to the patronage of Candour.–If it hath been anticipated, the testimony of many respectable persons, who saw it in manuscript as early as the year 1779, can obviate the imputation of plagiarism.

> THAT minds are not alike, full well I know,
> This truth each day's experience will show;
> To heights surprising some great sprits soar;
> With inborn strength mysterious depths explore;
> 5   Their eager gaze surveys the path of light,
> Confessed it stood to Newton's[1] piercing sight.
>
> Deep science, like a bashful maid retires;
> And but[2] the *ardent* breast her worth inspires;
> By perseverance the coy fair is won.
> 10   And Genius, led by Study, wears the crown.
>
> But some there are who wish not to improve,
> Who never can the path of knowledge love,
> Whose souls almost with the dull body one,
> With anxious care each mental pleasure shun;
> 15   Weak is the level'd, enervated mind,
> And but while here to vegetate design'd.
> The torpid spirit mingling with its clod,
> Can scarcely boast its origin from God;
> Stupidly dull–they move progressing on –
> 20   They eat, and drink, and all their work is done.
> While others, emulous of sweet applause,
> Industrious seek for each event a cause,
> Tracing the hidden springs whence knowledge flows,
> Which nature all in beauteous order shows,
>
> 25   Yet cannot I their sentiments imbibe,
> Who this distinction to the sex ascribe,
> As if woman's form must needs enroll,
> A weak, a servile, an inferiour soul;
> And that the guise of man must still proclaim,
> 30   Greatness of mind, and him, to be the same:
> Yet as the hours revolve fair proofs arise,
> Which the bright wreath of growing fame supplies;
> And in past times some men have *sunk* so *low*,

[†] Source: "Constantia." *Massachusetts Magazine; or, Monthly Museum Containing the Literature, History, Politics, Arts, Manners and Amusements of the Age* (1790): 132–35, 223–26.

[1] **Newton's:** Pertaining to Sir Isaac Newton (1642–1727), English scientist and philosopher. He broke up white light into the colors of the spectrum by means of a prism and likewise recombined colors.

[2] **And but:** And only.

That female records nothing *less* can show,
35   But imbecility is still confin'd,
And by the lordly sex to us consign'd;
They rob us of the power t'improve,
And then declare we only trifles love;
Yet haste the era, when the world shall know,
40   That such distinctions only dwell below;
The soul unfetter'd, to no sex confin'd,
Was for the abodes of cloudless day design'd.

Mean time we emulate their manly fires,
Through erudition all their thoughts inspire,
45   Yet nature with *equality* imparts,
And *noble passions*, swell e'en *female hearts.*

IS it upon mature consideration we adopt the idea, that nature is thus partial in her distributions? Is it indeed a fact, that she hath yielded to one half of the human species so unquestionable a mental superiority? I know that to both sexes elevated understandings, and the reverse, are common. But, suffer me to ask, in what the minds of females are so notoriously deficient, or unequal. May not the intellectual powers be ranged under these four heads—imagination, reason, memory and judgment. The province of imagination hath long since been surrendered up to us, and we have been crowned undoubted sovereigns of the regions of fancy. Invention is perhaps the most arduous effort of the mind; this branch of imagination hath been particularly ceded to us, and we have been time out of mind invested with that creative faculty. Observe the variety of fashions (here I bar the contemptuous smile) which distinguish and adorn the female world; how continually are they changing, insomuch that they almost render the wise man's assertion problematical, and we are ready to say, *there is something new under the sun.*[3] Now what a playfulness, what an exuberance of fancy, what strength of inventive imagination, doth this continual variation discover?[4] Again, it hath been observed, that if the turpitude of the conduct of our sex, hath been ever so enormous, so extremely ready are we, that the very first thought prevents us with an apology, so plausible, as to produce our actions even in an amiable light. Another instance of our creative powers, is our talent for slander; how ingenious are we at inventive scandal? what a formidable story can we in a moment fabricate merely from the force of a prolifick imagination? how many reputations, in the fertile brain of a female, have been utterly despoiled? how industrious are we at improving[5] a hint? Suspicion[6] how easily do we convert into conviction, and conviction, embellished by the power of eloquence, stalks abroad to the surprise and confusion of unsuspecting innocence. Perhaps it will be asked if I furnish these facts as instances of excellency in our sex. Certainly not; but as proofs of a creative

---

[3] *there is something new under the sun:* "There is no new thing under the sun" (Ecclesiastes 1.8).
[4] **discover:** Reveal.

[5] **improving:** Making use of.
[6] **Suspicion:** Imagine.

faculty, of a lively imagination. Assuredly great activity of mind is thereby discovered, and was this activity properly directed, what beneficial effects would follow. Is the needle and kitchen sufficient to employ the operations of a soul thus organized? I should conceive not. Nay, it is a truth that those very departments leave the intelligent principle vacant, and at liberty for speculation. Are we deficient in reason? we can only reason from what we know, and if an opportunity of acquiring knowledge hath been denied us, the inferiority of our sex cannot fairly be deduced from thence. Memory, I believe, will be allowed us in common, since every one's experience must testify, that a loquacious old woman is as frequently met with, as a communicative old man; their subjects are alike drawn from the fund of other times, and the transactions of their youth, or of maturer life, entertain, or perhaps fatigue you, in the evening of their lives. "But our judgment is not so strong—we do not distinguish so well."—Yet it may be questioned, from what doth this superiority, in this determining faculty of the soul, proceed. May we not trace its source in the difference of education, and continued advantages? Will it be said that the judgment of a male of two years old, is more sage than that of a female's of the same age? I believe the reverse is generally observed to be true. But from that period what partiality! how is the one exalted, and the other depressed, by the contrary modes of education which are adopted! the one is taught to aspire, and the other is early confined and limited. As their years increase, the sister must be wholly domesticated, while the brother is led by the hand through all the flowery paths of science. Grant that their minds are by nature equal, yet who shall wonder at the *apparent* superiority, if indeed custom becomes *second nature*; nay if it taketh place of nature, and that it doth the experience of each day will evince. At length arrived at womanhood, the uncultivated fair one feels a void, which the employments allotted her are by no means capable of filling. What can she do? to books she may not apply; or if she doth, *to those only of the novel kind,*[7] lest she merit the appellation of a *learned lady*; and what ideas have been affixed to this term, the observation of many can testify. Fashion, scandal, and sometimes what is still more reprehensible, are then called in to her relief; and who can say to what lengths the liberties she takes may proceed. Meantime she herself is most unhappy; she feels the want of a cultivated mind. Is she single, she in vain seeks to fill up time from sexual employments or amusements. Is she united to a person whose soul nature made equal to her own, education hath set him so far above her, that in those entertainments which are productive of such rational felicity, she is not qualified to accompany him. She experiences a mortifying consciousness of inferiority, which embitters every enjoyment. Doth the person to whom her adverse fate hath consigned her, possess a mind incapable of improvement, she is equally wretched, in being so closely connected with an individual whom she cannot but despise. Now, was she permitted the same instructors as her brother (with an eye however to their particular departments), for the employment of a rational mind an ample field would be opened. In astronomy she might catch a glimpse of the im-

---

[7] *to those only of the novel kind*: I.e., fiction.

mensity of the Deity, and thence she would form amazing conceptions of the august and supreme Intelligence. In geography she would admire Jehovah[8] in the midst of his benevolence; thus adapting this globe to the various wants and amusements of its inhabitants. In natural philosophy[9] she would adore the infinite majesty of heaven, clothed in condescension;[10] and as she traversed the reptile world, she would hail the goodness of a creating God. A mind, thus filled, would have little room for the trifles with which our sex are, with too much justice, accused of amusing themselves, and they would thus be rendered fit companions for those, who should one day wear them as their crown. Fashions, in their variety, would then give place to conjectures, which might perhaps conduce to the improvement of the literary world; and there would be no leisure for slander or detraction. Reputation would not then be blasted, but serious speculations would occupy the lively imaginations of the sex. Unnecessary visits would be precluded, and that custom would only be indulged by way of relaxation, or to answer the demands of consanguinity and friendship. Females would become discreet, their judgments would be invigorated, and their partners for life being circumspectly chosen, an unhappy Hymen[11] would then be as rare, as is now the reverse…

Will it be urged that those acquirements would supersede our domestick duties. I answer that every requisite in female economy[12] is easily attained; and, with truth I can add, that when once attained, they require no further *mental attention*. Nay, while we are pursuing the needle, or the superintendency of the family, I repeat, that our minds are at full liberty for reflection; that imagination may exert itself in full vigor; and that if a just foundation is early laid, our ideas will then be worthy of rational beings. If we were industrious we might easily find time to arrange them upon paper, or should avocations press too hard for such an indulgence, the hours allotted for conversation would at least become more refined and rational. Should it be vociferated, "Your domestick employments are sufficient—" I would calmly ask, is it reasonable, that a candidate for immortality, for the joys of heaven, an intelligent being, who is to spend an eternity in contemplating the works of the Deity, should at present be so degraded, as to be allowed no other ideas, than those which are suggested by the mechanism of a pudding, or the sewing the seams of a garment? Pity that all such censurers of female improvement do not go one step further, and deny their future existence; to be confident they surely ought…

Yes, ye lordly, ye haughty sex, our souls are by nature equal to yours; the same breath of God animates, enlivens, and invigorates us; and that we are not fallen lower than yourselves, let those witness who have greatly towered above the various discouragements by which they have been so heavily oppressed; and though I am unacquainted with the list of celebrated characters on either side, yet from the observa-

---

[8] **Jehovah:** The principal and personal name of God in the Hebrew Scriptures.
[9] **natural philosophy:** Natural science.
[10] **condescension:** Voluntary assumption of equality with a person regarded as inferior.

[11] **Hymen:** In Greek and Roman mythology, the God of marriage, usually represented as a young man carrying a torch and veil.
[12] **female economy:** Housekeeping.

tions I have made in the contracted circle in which I have moved, I dare confidently believe, that from the commencement of time to the present day, there hath been as many females, as males, who, by the *mere force of natural powers*, have merited the crown of applause; who, *thus unassisted*, have seized the wreath of fame. I know there are [those] who assert, that as the animal powers of the one sex are superiour, of course their mental faculties also must be stronger; thus attributing strength of mind to the transient organization of this earth born tenement.[13] But if this reasoning is just, man must content to yield the palm to many of the brute creation, since by not a few of his brethren of the field, he is far surpassed in bodily strength. Moreover, was this argument admitted, it would prove too much, for occular demonstration evinceth, that there are many robust masculine ladies, and effeminate gentlemen. Yet I fancy that Mr. Pope[14] though clogged with an enervated body, and distinguished by a diminutive stature, could nevertheless lay claim to greatness of soul; and perhaps there are many other instances which might be adduced[15] to combat so unphilosophical an opinion. Do we not often see, that when the clay built tabernacle[16] is well nigh dissolved, when it is just ready to mingle with the parent soil, the immortal inhabitant aspires to, and even attaineth heights the most sublime, and which were before wholly unexplored. Besides, were we to grant that animal strength proved any thing, taking into consideration the accustomed impartiality of nature, we should be induced to imagine, that she had invested the female mind with superiour strength as an equivalent for the bodily powers of man. But waving this however palpable advantage, for *equality only*, we wish to contend…

I AM aware that there are many passages in the sacred oracles which seem to give the advantage to the other sex; but I consider all these as wholly metaphorical. Thus David[17] was a man after God's own heart, yet see him enervated by his licentious passions! behold him following Uriah[18] to the death, and shew me wherein could consist the immaculate Being's complacency. Listen to the curses which Job[19] bestoweth upon the day of his nativity, and tell me where is his perfection, where his patience—literally it existed not. David and Job were types[20] of him who was to come; and the superiority of man, as exhibited in scripture, being also emblematical, all arguments deduced from thence, of course fall to the ground. The exquisite delicacy of the female mind proclaimeth the exactness[21] of its texture, while its nice[22] sense of honour announceth its innate, its native grandeur. And indeed, in one respect, the preeminence seems to be tacitly allowed us; for after an education which

---

[13] **tenement:** Dwelling-place.

[14] **Mr. Pope:** Alexander Pope (1688–1744), a famous English poet and satirist.

[15] **adduced:** To bring forward in a statement, to cite, to allege.

[16] **tabernacle:** The body, which houses the soul.

[17] **David:** The second king of Israel. See 1 Samuel 16:1 to 1 Kings 2:11.

[18] **Uriah:** One of King David's generals. David had him executed to conceal his affair with Uriah's wife,

Bathsheba, while Uriah was away at war (see 2 Samuel 11:1–25).

[19] **Job:** A patriarch whose faith is tested by God by many misfortunes. Although his faith survives many testings, he curses the day he was born (see Job 3).

[20] **types:** Prefigurations. In medieval exegesis known as typology, Old Testament persons and events took on their full meaning in the New Testament. Job and David are thus, in their suffering, prefigurations of Jesus.

[21] **exactness:** High finish or quality.

[22] **nice:** Refined.

limits and confines, and employments and recreations which naturally tend to ener-vate the body, and debilitate the mind; after we have from early youth been adorned with ribbons, and other gewgaws,[23] dressed out like the ancient victims previous to a sacrifice, being taught by the care of our parents in collecting the most showy ma-terials that the ornamenting our exteriour ought to be the principal object of our attention; after, I say, fifteen years thus spent, we are introduced into the world, amid the united adulation of every beholder. Praise is sweet to the soul; we are immedi-ately intoxicated by large draughts of flattery, which being plentifully administered, is to the pride of our hearts the most acceptable incense. It is expected that with the other sex we should commence immediate war, and that we should triumph over the machinations of the most artful. We must be constantly upon our guard; pru-dence and discretion must be our characteristicks; and we must rise superiour to, and obtain a complete victory over those who have been long adding to the native strength of their minds, by an unremitted study of men and books, and who have, moreover, conceived from the loose characters which they have seen portrayed in the extensive variety of their reading, a most contemptible opinion of the sex. Thus unequal, we are, notwithstanding, forced to the combat, and the infamy which is consequent upon the smallest deviation in our conduct, proclaims the high idea which was formed of our native strength; and thus, indirectly at least, is the prefer-ence acknowledged to be our due. And if we are allowed an equality of acquirement, let serious studies equally employ our minds, and we will bid our souls arise to equal strength. We will meet upon even ground, the despot man; we will rush with alacrity to the combat, and, crowned by success, we shall then answer the exalted expecta-tions which are formed. Though sensibility, soft compassion, and gentle commisera-tion, are inmates in the female bosom, yet against every deep laid art, altogether fearless of the event, we will set them in array; for assuredly the wreath of victory will encircle the spotless brow. If we meet an equal, a sensible friend, we will reward him with the hand of amity, and through life we will be assiduous to promote his happi-ness; but from every deep laid scheme for our ruin, retiring into ourselves, amid the flowery paths of science, we will indulge in all the refined and sentimental pleasures of contemplation. And should it still be urged, that the studies thus insisted upon would interfere with our more peculiar department,[24] I must further reply, that *early hours*, and close application, will do wonders; and to her who is from the first dawn of reason taught to fill up time rationally, both the requisites will be easy. I grant that niggard fortune is too generally unfriendly to the mind, and that much of that valu-able treasure, time, is necessarily expended upon the wants of the body; but it should be remembered; that in embarrassed circumstances our companions have as little leisure for literary improvement, as is afforded to us; for most certainly their provi-dent care is at least as requisite as our exertions. Nay, we have even more leisure for sedentary pleasures, as our avocations are more retired, much less laborious, and; as

[23] **gewgaws:** Trinkets.
[24] **peculiar department:** I.e., duties belonging particularly to women.

hath been observed, by no means require that avidity of attention which is proper to the employments of the other sex. In high life, or, in other words, where the parties are in possession of affluence, the objection respecting time is wholly obviated, and of course falls to the ground; and it may also be repeated, that many of those hours which are at present swallowed up in fashion and scandal, might be redeemed, were we habituated to useful reflections. But in one respect, O ye arbiters of our fate! we confess that the superiority is indubitably yours; you are by nature formed for our protectors; we pretend not to vie with you in bodily strength; upon this point we will never contend for victory. Shield us then, we beseech you, from external evils, and in return *we* will transact *your* domestick affairs. Yes, *your*, for are you not equally interested in those matters with ourselves? Is not the elegancy of neatness as agreeable to your fight as to ours; is not the well favoured viand[25] equally delightful to your taste; and doth not your sense of hearing suffer as much, from the discordant sounds prevalent in an ill regulated family, produced by the voices of children and many *et ceteras*?

CONSTANTIA.

By way of supplement to the foregoing pages, I subjoin the following extract from a letter, wrote to a friend in the December of 1780.

AND now assist me, O thou genius of my sex, while I undertake the arduous task of endeavouring to combat that vulgar, that almost universal errour, which hath, it seems, enlisted even Mr. P– under its banners. The superiority of your sex hath, I grant, been time out of mind esteemed a truth incontrovertible; in consequence of which persuasion, every plan of education hath been calculated to establish this favourite tenet. Not long since; weak and presuming as I was, I amused myself with selecting some arguments from nature, reason, and experience; against this so generally received idea: I confess that to sacred testimonies[26] I had not recourse. I held them to be merely metaphorical, and thus regarding them, I could not persuade myself that there was any propriety in bringing them to decide in this *very important debate*. However, as you, sir, confine yourself entirely to the sacred oracles, I mean to bend the whole of my artillery against those supposed proofs, which you have from thence provided, and from which you have formed an intrenchment *apparently* so invulnerable. And first, to begin with our great progenitors;[27] but here, suffer me to premise, that it is for mental strength I mean to contend, for with respect to animal powers, I yield them undisputed to that sex, which enjoys them in common with the lion, the tyger, and many other beasts of prey; therefore your observations respecting the *rib, under the arm, at a distance from the head*, &c. &c.[28] in no sort militate against my view. Well, but the woman was first in the transgression. Strange how

---

[25] **viand:** An article of food, provisions, or victuals.
[26] **sacred testimonies:** The Bible.
[27] **progenitors:** Ancestors; here, Adam and Eve.

[28] ***rib, ..., &c. &c:*** "And the rib, which the Lord God had taken from man, made he a woman, and brought her unto the man" (Genesis 2.22).

blind *self love* renders you men; were you not wholly absorbed in a partial admiration of your own abilities, you would long since have acknowledged the force of what I am now going to urge. It is true some ignoramuses have absurdly enough informed us, that the beauteous fair of paradise, was seduced from her obedience, by a malignant demon, *in the guise of a baleful serpent*; but we, who are better informed, know that the fallen spirit presented himself to her view, a *shining angel still*; for thus, saith the cricks in the Hebrew tongue, ought the word to be rendered.[29] Let us examine her motive—Hark! the seraph[30] declares that she shall attain a perfection of knowledge; for is there aught which is not comprehended under one or other of the terms *good* and *evil*. It doth not appear that she was governed by any one sensual appetite; but merely by a desire of adorning her mind; a laudable ambition fired her soul, and a thirst for knowledge impelled the predilection so fatal in its consequences. Adam could not plead the same deception; assuredly he was not deceived; nor ought we to admire his superiour strength, or wonder at his sagacity, when we so often confess that example is much more influential than precept. His gentle partner stood before him, a melancholy instance of the direful effects of disobedience; he saw her not possessed of that wisdom which she had fondly hoped to obtain, but he beheld the once blooming female, disrobed of that innocence, which had heretofore rendered her so lovely. To him then deception became impossible, as he had proof positive of the fallacy of the argument, which the deceiver had suggested. What then could be his inducement to burst the barriers, and to fly directly in the face of that command, which *immediately* from the mouth of deity *he* had received, since, I say, he could not plead that fascinating stimulous, the accumulation of knowledge, as indisputable conviction was so visibly portrayed before him. What mighty cause impelled him to sacrifice myriads of beings yet unborn, and by one impious act, which *he saw* would be productive of such fatal effects, entail undistinguished ruin upon a race of beings, which he was yet to produce. Blush, ye vaunters of fortitude; ye boasters of resolution; ye haughty lords of the creation; blush when ye remember, that he was influenced by no other motive than a bare pusillanimous attachment to a woman! by sentiments so exquisitely soft, that all his sons have, from that period, when they have designed to degrade them, described as highly feminine. Thus it should seem, that all the arts of the grand deceiver (since means adequate to the purpose are, I conceive, invariably pursued) were requisite to mislead our general mother, while the father of mankind forfeited his own, and relinquished the happiness of posterity, merely in compliance with the blandishments of a female. The subsequent subjection the apostle Paul explains as a figure; after enlarging upon the subject, he adds, *"This is a great mystery; but I speak concerning Christ and the church."*[31] Now we know with what consummate wisdom the unerring father of eternity hath formed his plans; all the types which he hath displayed, he hath permitted *materially* to fail, in the very virtue for which *they* were famed. The reason for this is obvious, we might otherwise mistake his economy, and render that honour to the

---

[29] *in the ... rendered:* The earliest connection with Satan and light is in Isaiah 14.12: "How are thou fallen from heaven, O Lucifer, son of the morning!"

[30] **seraph:** In the Old Testament, a type of angel that possesses six wings, hands, feet, and a voice.
[31] *"This is a ... church":* Ephesians 5:32.

creature, which is due only to the creator. I know that Adam was a figure of him who was to come.[32] The grace contained in this figure, is the reason of my rejoicing, and while I am very far from prostrating before the shadow, I yield joyfully in all things the preeminence to the second federal head.[33] Confiding faith is prefigured by Abraham, yet he exhibits a contrast to affiance,[34] when he says of his fair companion, she is my sister.[35] Gentleness was the characteristick of Moses,[36] yet he hesitated not to reply to Jehovah himself, with unsaintlike tongue he murmured at the waters of strife, and with rash hands he broke the tables,[37] which were inscribed by the finger of divinity. David, dignified with the title of the man after God's own heart, and yet how stained was his life. Solomon[38] was celebrated for wisdom, but folly is written in legible characters upon his almost every action. Lastly, let us turn our eyes to man in the aggregate. He is manifested as the figure of strength, but that we may not regard him as any thing more than a figure, his soul is formed in no sort superiour, but every way equal to the mind of her, who is the emblem of weakness, and whom he hails the gentle companion of his better days.

—1790

Phillis Wheatley ca. 1753–1784

Destined to become the first published woman of African descent and the widely recognized founder of African American literature, Phillis Wheatley was born somewhere in West Africa, probably between present-day Gambia and Ghana. She was taken to Boston aboard the slave ship *Phillis* in 1761 and bought by John and Susanna Wheatley, who employed her as a domestic servant. Encouraged by her mistress, Phillis quickly became literate and began writing poetry that soon found its way into Boston newspapers. Phillis Wheatley gained international recognition with her 1770 funeral elegy on the death of the evangelist George Whitefield, addressed to his English patron, Selina Hastings, Countess of Huntingdon, and published in London and Boston in 1771. By 1772 Wheatley had written enough poems to enable her to try to capitalize on her growing transatlantic reputation by producing a book of previously published and new verse. Unable to find a publisher in Boston, Susanna and Phillis Wheatley successfully sought a London publisher and Huntingdon's patronage. Having spent several weeks in London with her master's son in 1773 before the publication there of her *Poems on Various Subjects: Religious and Moral,* Phillis

---

[32] **I know that Adam ... to come:** Adam prefigures Jesus.

[33] **the second federal head:** Jesus; he made a new Covenant of Faith with man after Adam broke God's Covenant of Works. "Federal" means "compact."

[34] **affiance:** Plighted faith; marriage.

[35] **Abraham ... my sister:** This refers to verses in the Hebrew scriptures Genesis 12:10-20, where Abraham, the first patriarch and progenitor of the Hebrews, is about to enter Egypt with his wife and fears for his life, saying to her: "Say, I pray thee, thou art my sister: that it may be well with me for thy sake; and my soul shall live because of thee" (12.13).

[36] **Moses:** The lawgiver who led the Israelites out of Egypt; he is described as "very meek, above all the men which were upon the face of the earth" (Numbers 12.3).

[37] **tables:** The tablets containing the Ten Commandments (Exodus 32.19).

[38] **Solomon:** King of Israel (tenth century B.C.E.). Although he was famous for his riches and his wisdom, he worshipped false gods and failed to keep God's commandments (see 1 Kings 11.1-10).

Wheatley returned to Boston to nurse her ailing mistress. Once there, she was soon freed, "at the desire of my friends in England." Wheatley's *Poems* earned the praise of fellow black writers Jupiter Hammon and Ignatius Sancho. Sancho referred to her as a "genius in bondage." Her literary achievements are even more remarkable when we recall that the contents of her *Poems* were all written while she was a teenager. Even Thomas Jefferson begrudgingly acknowledged her literary efforts. Many subsequent critics have found subtle challenges to slavery and racism expressed in Wheatley's poetry, which became increasingly explicitly "American" in tone and content once hostilities between Britain and its colonies broke out in the American Revolution. The last years of Wheatley's life were marked by personal and financial loss. On April 1, 1778, she married John Peters, a free black who subsequently changed occupations frequently and was often in debt. They had three children, who all died very young. Phillis Wheatley Peters never found a publisher for her proposed second volume of poems, even though her poems continued to be praised and published in Britain. She died in abject poverty in Boston on December 5, 1784, and was buried in an unmarked grave with her youngest child on December 8.

Further Reading   Vincent Carretta, "Introduction," in Phillis Wheatley, *Complete Writings*, ed. Vincent Carreta (2001); Phillip M. Richards, "Phillis Wheatley and Literary Americanization," *American Quarterly* 44 (1992); William H. Robinson, *Phillis Wheatley and Her Writings* (1984); Frank Shuffleton, "On Her Own Footing: Phillis Wheatley in Freedom," in *"Genius in Bondage": A Critical Anthology of the Literature of the Early Black Atlantic*, eds. Vincent Carretta and Philip Gould (2001); Carla Wilcox, "Wheatley's Turns of Praise: Heroic Entrapment and the Paradox of Revolution," *American Literature* 67 (1995).

—*Vincent Carretta, University of Maryland, College Park*

From Poems on Various Subjects: Religious and Moral[†]

On being brought from AFRICA to AMERICA.

TWAS mercy brought me from my *Pagan* land,
Taught my benighted soul to understand
That there's a God, that there's a *Saviour* too:
Once I redemption neither sought nor knew,
5   Some view our sable[1] race with scornful eye,
"Their colour is a diabolic die."
Remember, *Christians, Negroes*, black as *Cain*,[2]
May be refin'd, and join th' angelic train.

[†] Source: *Poems on Various Subjects, Religious and Moral* (London: Archibald Bell, 1773); the original edition contains notes by an editor; for the purpose of this selection, these notes will be placed in quotation marks indicated thus: [ed].

[1] **sable:** Black.
[2] **Cain:** One of Adam's and Eve's sons who slew his brother Abel and was therefore "marked" by God (see Genesis 4.1–15). This mark has sometimes been interpreted to be the origin of dark-skinned people.

On Recollection

MNEME[3] begin. Inspire, ye sacred nine,
Your vent'rous *Afric* in her great design.
Mneme, immortal pow'r, I trace thy spring:
Assist my strains, while I thy glories sing:
5 The acts of long departed years, by thee
Recover'd, in due order rang'd we see:
Thy pow'r the long-forgotten calls from night,
That sweetly plays before the *fancy's* sight.
Mneme in our nocturnal visions pours
10 The ample treasure of her secret stores;
Swift from above the wings her silent flight
Through *Phoebe's* realms, fair regent of the night;
And, in her pomp of images display'd,
To the high-raptur'd poet gives her aid,
15 Through the unbounded regions of the mind,
Diffusing light celestial and refin'd.
The heav'nly *phantom* paints the actions done
By ev'ry tribe beneath the rolling sun.

Mneme, enthron'd within the human breast,
20 Has vice condemn'd, and ev'ry virtue blest.
How sweet the sound when we her plaudit hear?
Sweeter than music to the ravish'd ear,
Sweeter than *Maro's*[4] entertaining strains
Resounding through the groves, and hills, and plains.
25 But how is *Mneme* dreaded by the race,
Who scorn her warnings and despise her grace?
By her unveil'd each horrid crime appears,
Her awful hand a cup of wormwood bears.
Days, years mispent, O what a hell of woe!
30 Hers the worst tortures that our souls can know.

Now eighteen years their destin'd course have run,
In fast succession round the central sun.
How did the follies of that period pass
Unnotic'd, but behold them writ in brass!
35 In Recollection see them fresh return,
And sure 'tis mine to be asham'd, and mourn.

O *Virtue,* smiling in immortal green,
Do thou exert thy pow'r, and change the scene;
Be thine employ to guide my future days,
40 And mine to pay the tribute of my praise.

----

[3] **MNEME:** The Muse of memory, or remembrance, in Greek mythology.
[4] ***Maro's:*** Maro is another name for the ancient Roman poet Virgil (70 B.C.E.–19 B.C.E.).

Of *Recollection* such the pow'r enthron'd
In ev'ry breast, and thus her pow'r is own'd.
The wretch, who dar'd the vengeance of the skies,
At last awakes in horror and surprise,
45   By her alarm'd, he sees impending fate,
He howls in anguish, and repents too late.
But O! what peace, what joys are hers t' impart
To ev'ry holy, ev'ry upright heart!
Thrice blest the man, who, in her sacred shrine,
50   Feels himself shelter'd from the wrath divine!

A Farewell to America. To Mrs. S. W.[5]

I.

DIEU, *New-England's* smiling meads,
    Adieu, the flow'ry plain:
I leave thine op'ning charms, O spring,
    And tempt the roaring main.

II.

5   In vain for me the flow'rets rise,
    And boast their gaudy pride,
While here beneath the northern skies
    I mourn for *health* deny'd.

III.

Celestial maid of rosy hue,
10   O let me feel thy reign!
I languish till thy face I view,
    Thy vanish'd joys regain.

IV.

Susanna mourns, nor can I bear
    To see the crystal show'r,
15   Or mark the tender falling tear
    At sad departure's hour;

V.

Not unregarding can I see
    Her soul with grief opprest:
But let no sighs, no groans for me,
20   Steal from her pensive breast

---

[5] **Mrs. S. W.:** Susanna Wheatley, Phillis's mistress. Phillis was leaving for England to promote her poetry and health. In England, Lord Mansfield had just decided in the Somerset case of 1772, ruling that slaves escaped from their masters in Britain would not have to be returned to slavery. Wheatley did return to Boston and was freed in 1774.

VI.

In vain the feather'd warblers sing,
    In vain the garden blooms,
And on the bosom of the spring
    Breathes out her sweet perfumes.

VII.

25 While for *Britannia's* distant shore
    We sweep the liquid plain,
And with astonish'd eyes explore
    The wide-extended main.

VIII.

Lo! *Health* appears! celestial dame!
30   Complacent and serene,
With *Hebe's* mantle o'er her Frame,[6]
    With soul-delighting mein.

IX.

To mark the vale where *London* lies
    With misty vapours crown'd,
35 Which cloud *Aurora's* thousand dyes,
    And veil her charms around.

X.

Why, *Phoebus*,[7] moves thy car so slow?
    So slow thy rising ray?
Give us the famous town to view,
40   Thou glorious king of day!

XI.

For thee, *Britannia,* I resign
    New-England's smiling fields;
To view again her charms divine,
    What joy the prospect yields!

XII.

45 But thou! Temptation hence away,
    With all thy fatal train,
Nor once seduce my soul away,
    By thine enchanting strain.

---

[6] **With *Hebe's* mantle o'er her Frame:** In Greek mythology, Hebe was the Greek goddess of eternal youth. She has also been associated with freeing people from bondage.

[7] ***Phoebus:*** The sun-god in Classicist European poetry, where Phoebus and his car (chariot) often figure as a metaphor for the sun.

XIII.

Thrice happy they, whose heav'nly shield
50   Secures their souls from harms,
And fell *Temptation* on the field
        Of all its pow'r disarms!

—*Boston, May 7, 1773.*

To His Excellency
George Washington[†][1]

Sir,

I have taken the freedom to address your Excellency in the enclosed poem, and entreat
your acceptance, though I am not insensible of its inaccuracies. Your being appointed
by the Grand Continental Congress to be Generalissimo of the armies of North America, together with the fame of your virtues, excite sensations not easy to suppress. Your
generosity, therefore, I presume, will pardon the attempt. Wishing your Excellency all
possible success in the great cause you are so generously engaged in. I am,

Your Excellency's most obedient humble servant,

Phillis Wheatley

1776

Celestial choir! enthron'd in realms of light,
Columbia's[2] scenes of glorious toils I write.
While freedom's cause her anxious breast alarms,
She flashes dreadful in refulgent arms.
5   See mother earth her offspring's fate bemoan,
And nations gaze at scenes before unknown!
See the bright beams of heaven's revolving light
Involved in sorrows and veil of night!

The goddess comes, she moves divinely fair,
10   Olive and laurel bind her golden hair:
Wherever shines this native of the skies,
Unnumber'd charms and recent graces rise.

Muse! bow propitious while my pen relates
How pour her armies through a thousand gates,
15   As when Eolus[3] heaven's fair face deforms,
Enwrapp'd in tempest and a night of storms;
Astonish'd ocean feels the wild uproar,
The refluent surges beat the sounding shore;
Or thick as leaves in Autumn's golden reign,

---

† Source: *Pennsylvania Gazette* (April 1776).
[1] **George Washington** (1732–1799): A famous general of the Seven Years War, Washington would lead the thirteen colonies' Continental Army to victory over the British and become the first president of the United States.
[2] **Columbia's:** Columbia is another name for America.
[3] **Eolus:** Or Aeolus, the classical god of the winds.

20 Such, and so many, moves the warrior's train.
In bright array they seek the work of war,
Where high unfurl'd the ensign waves in air.
Shall I to Washington their praise recite?
Enough thou know'st them in the fields of fight.
25 Thee, first in peace and honours,—we demand
The grace and glory of thy martial band.
Fam'd for thy valour, for thy virtues more,
Hear every tongue thy guardian aid implore!

One century scarce perform'd its destined round,
30 When Gallic powers Columbia's fury found;[4]
And so may you, whoever dares disgrace
The land of freedom's heaven-defended race!
Fix'd are the eyes of nations on the scales,
For in their hopes Columbia's arm prevails.
35 Anon Britannia droops the pensive head,
While round increase the rising hills of dead.
Ah! cruel blindness to Columbia's state!
Lament thy thirst of boundless power too late.

Proceed, great chief, with virtue on thy side,
40 Thy ev'ry action let the goddess guide.
A crown, a mansion, and a throne that shine,
With gold unfading, WASHINGTON! be thine.

—1774

Letter to Reverend Samson Occum[†1]

Rev'd and honor'd Sir,

I have this Day received your obliging kind Epistle, and am greatly satisfied with your Reasons respecting the Negroes, and think highly reasonable what you offer in Vindication of their natural Rights: Those that invade them cannot be insensible that the divine Light is chasing away the thick Darkness which broods over the Land of Africa; and the Chaos which has reign'd so long, is converting into beautiful Order, and [r]eveals more and more clearly, the glorious Dispensation of civil and religious Liberty, which are so inseparably Limited, that there is little or no Enjoyment of one Without the other: Otherwise, perhaps, the Israelites had been less solicitous for their Freedom from Egyptian slavery; I do not say they would have been contented without it, by no means, for in every human Breast, God has implanted a Principle, which we call Love of Freedom; it is impatient of Oppression, and pants

---

[4] **Gallic powers Columbia's fury found:** A reference to the French and Indian War (or Seven Years' War) 1756–1763, in which Britain and the colonial militia defeated France. "Gallic" is the Latinate word for "French."

[†] Source: *The Connecticut Gazette*, March 11, 1774.
[1] **Samson Occum** (1723–1792): A Mohegan Indian who became a student of the missionary Eleazar Wheelock, a Presbyterian minister, and a missionary.

for Deliverance; and by the Leave of our modern Egyptians I will assert, that the same Principle lives in us. God grant Deliverance in his own Way and Time, and get his honour upon all those whose Avarice impels them to countenance and help forward vile Calamities of their fellow Creatures. This I desire not for their Hurt, but to convince them of the strange Absurdity of their Conduct whose Words and Actions are so diametrically opposite. How well the Cry for Liberty, and the reverse Disposition for the exercise of oppressive Power over others agree, —

I humbly think it does not require the Penetration of a Philosopher to determine.—

—1774

Jupiter Hammon   1711–ca. 1806

Jupiter Hammon was born a slave on Long Island, New York. Having received a rudimentary education at a school built on the estate on which he served and having a propensity for Christian spirituality, he began to write. In 1760, he published his first poem, "An evening Thought: Salvation by Christ, with Penitential Cries," which makes him the first published black poet in British America. When his owner, Henry Lloyd, died in 1763, Hammon became the property of Joseph Lloyd, a patriot who was obliged to flee from British troops to Stamford and later Hartford, Connecticut, with his household and slaves. There Hammon published more of his poetry and some of his sermons and addresses, including "An Address to Miss Phillis Wheatly [sic], Ethiopian Poetess, in Boston, who came from Africa at eight year of age and soon became acquainted with the Gospel of Jesus Christ" (1778).

Further Reading   Joanna Brooks, *American Lazarus: Religion and the Rise of African-American and Native American Literatures* (2003); Dickson D. Bruce, *The Origins of African American Literature, 1680–1865* (2001); Vincent Carretta and Philip Gould, eds., *Genius in Bondage: Literature of the Early Black Atlantic* (2001); Sandra O'Neale, *Jupiter Hammon and the Biblical Beginnings of African American Literature* (1993).

An Address to Miss Phillis Wheatly [sic], Ethiopian Poetess, in Boston, who came from Africa at eight year of age, and soon became acquainted with the gospel of Jesus Christ[†]

Miss **Wheatly**, pray give have to express as follows:

1
O come you pious youth I adore
The wisdom of thy God,
In bringing thee from distant shore,   ECCLES. XII.
To learn his holy word.

[†] Source: Jupiter Hammon, *An Address to Miss Phillis Wheatly* (Hartford, CT, 1778).

2

Thou mightst been left behind,
Amidst a dark abode;   PSAL. CXXXV, 2, 3.
God's tender mercy still combin'd,
Thou hast the holy word.

3

Fair wisdom's ways are paths of peace,
And they that walk therein,
Shall reap the joys that never cease,   PSAL. II. 2;
And Christ shall be their king.   PROV. III, 7.

4

God's tender mercy brought thee here,
Tost o'er the raging main;   PSAL. CIII, I, 3, 4.
In Christian faith thou hast a share,
Worth all the gold of Spain.[1]

5

While thousands tossed by the sea,
And others settled down,   DEATH
God's tender mercy set thee free,
From dangers still unknown.

6

That thou a pattern still might be,
To youth of Boston town,   2 COR V.10.
The blessed Jesus set thee free,
From every sinful wound.

7

The blessed Jesus, who came down,
Unvail'd his sacred face,   ROM. V, 21.
To cleanse the soul of every wound,
And give repenting grace.

8

That we poor sinners may obtain
The pardon of our sin;   PSAL. XXXIV, 6, 7, 8
Dear blessed Jesus now constrain,
And bring us flocking in.

9

Come you, Phillis, now aspire,
And seek the living God,   MATTH. VII, 7, 8.
So step by step thou mayst go higher,
Till perfect in the word.

---

[1] **all the gold of Spain:** Spain's exploits in gold and other minerals in the New World were proverbial.

10
While thousands mov'd to distant shore,
And others left behind,   PSAL. LXXXIX, I.
The blessed Jesus still adore,
40   Implant this in thy mind.

11
Thou hast left the heathen shore,
Thro' mercy of the Lord;   PSAL. XXXIV, I, 2, 3.
Among the heathen live no more,
Come magnify thy God.

12
45   I pray the living God may be,
The shepherd of thy soul;   PSAL. LXXX, 1, 2, 3.
His tender mercies still are free,
His mysteries to unfold.

13
Thou, Phillis, when thou hunger hast,
50   Or pantest for thy God;   PSAL. XIII, 1, 2, 3.
Jesus Christ is thy relief,
Thou hast the holy word.

14
The bounteous mercies of the Lord,
Are hid beyond the sky,   PSAL. XIV, 10, 11.
55   And holy souls that love his word,
Shall taste them when they die.

15
These bounteous mercies are from God,
The merits of his Son;   PSAL. XXXIV. 15.
The humble soul that loves his word,
60   He chooses for his own.

16
Come, dear Phillis, be advis'd,
To drink Samaria's flood;   JOHN IV, 13, 14.
There nothing is that shall suffice
But Christ's redeming blood.

17
65   While thousands muse with earthly toys,
And range about the street,   MATTH. VI, 33.
Dear Phillis, seek for heaven's joys,
Where we do hope to meet.

18
When God shall send his summons down,
70   And number saints together,   PSAL. CXVI, 15.

Blest angels chant, (triumphant sound)
Come live with me for ever.

19

The humble soul shall fly to God,
And leave the things of time,   MATTH. V, 3, 8.
Start forth as 'twere at the first word,
To taste things more divine.

75

20

Behold! the soul shall waft away,
Whene'er we come to die,   I COR. XV, 51, 52, 53.
And leave its cottage made of clay,
In twinkling of an eye.

80

21

Now glory be to the Most High,
United praises given,   PSAL. CL, 6.
By all on earth, incessantly,
And all the host of heav'n.

Composed by JUPITER HAMMON, a Negro Man belonging to Mr. Joseph Lloyd, of
Queen's Village, on Long-Island, now in Hartford.

—1778

François Dominique Toussaint L'Ouverture ca. 1743–1803

Born into slavery in northern Saint Domingue, Toussaint L'Ouverture became the
leader of the most successful slave revolution in history, which eventually led to the
establishment of Haiti, the world's first free black republic. Although L'Ouverture
died before he could see what had once been France's wealthiest colony reborn as an
independent state, his reputation as a great liberator and formidable military strate-
gist—"first and greatest of West Indians," as C. L. R. James called him—was secured
for posterity by writers in Europe and the Americas throughout the nineteenth and
twentieth centuries. Freed by his master sometime during the 1770s, L'Ouverture
became a coffee farmer, leasing land and slaves to work his plantation. In 1791, when
he was over forty years old, he joined with a group of insurgent slaves, soon rising to
command as a general in the revolution that eradicated colonial slavery throughout
the island. But in 1794, for reasons that historians can only speculate about,
L'Ouverture changed sides and joined with the French, becoming the first black general to serve in the French army and defeating both the Spanish and British forces
vying for control of Hispaniola. Although he has been criticized for harshly curtail-
ing the liberty of ex-slaves in order to ensure the continuation of the plantation
economy, it is also true that, as Laurent Dubois notes, "this was a failure he shared
with the leaders of every other post-emancipation society in the Atlantic world."
During this period, L'Ouverture was also consolidating his own authority, weakening
the control of colonial French Commissioners while nominally continuing to serve
as loyal subject of France. In 1799, Napoleon took power in the wake of the French
Revolution and soon determined to reinstate the colonial system of slavery in Saint

Domingue and to eliminate, as he put it, "this gilded African" leading the island. In 1802, new French troops arrived, and L'Ouverture was captured. He died in a French prison in 1803. Rather than including L'Ouverture's more widely known proclamations and letters, this text represents his little discussed *Memoir,* produced during his captivity in France. Describing the events of 1802 leading up to his arrest, the *Memoir* is L'Ouverture's account of his betrayal by the very government he had served so brilliantly—and his attempt to insert his own voice into the official history of the revolution. Said to have been a great reader of histories, biographies, and military memoirs, L'Ouverture did not, however, record any of his surviving work in his own hand, instead dictating it in French and Creole to secretaries. The *Memoir* itself was apparently transcribed by Martial Besse, a mixed-race officer in the army of Saint Domingue who was imprisoned with L'Ouverture—and since its first appearance in French, there have been accusations that L'Ouverture was not the true author of this highly mediated work. Yet we might more productively place this text within the Atlantic history of slavery, using it to raise questions about how we define authorship, authentication, and oral versus written forms in our studies of American literature. First published in Paris in 1853, during a wave of republican and anti-Napoleonic sentiment, the *Memoir* was then translated into English by John Relly Beard, whose text appears here. Beard's translation was first published by James Redpath in Boston in 1863—precisely when white northerners in the United States were debating the efficacy of black soldiers and officers in the Union troops. As Redpath put it in his preface, "'Are the Negroes fit for Soldiers? . . . Are Negroes fit for Officers?' We are entering on that debate now. The Life of Louverture may help to end it."

Further Reading J. R. Beard, *Toussaint L'Ouverture: A Biography and Autobiography* (1863); Daniel Desormeaux, "The First of the (Black) Memorialists: Toussaint Louverture," *Yale French Studies*, No. 107 (Spring 2005); Laurent Dubois, *Avengers of the New World: The Story of the Haitian Revolution* (2004); C. L. R. James, *The Black Jacobins: Toussaint Louverture and the San Domingo Revolution* (1938).

—*Anna Brickhouse, University of Virginia*

From The Memoir[†]

It is my duty to render to the French Government an exact account of my conduct. I shall relate the facts with all the simplicity and frankness of an old soldier, adding to them the reflections that naturally suggest themselves. In short, I shall tell the truth, though it be against myself.

The colony of Saint Domingo,[1] of which I was commander, enjoyed the greatest tranquility; agriculture and commerce flourished there. The island had attained a degree of splendor which it had never before seen. And all this—I dare to say—was my work. . . .

[†] Source: John Relly Beard, *Toussaint L'Ouverture: A Biography and Autobiography* (Boston: James Redpath Publisher, 1863).
[1] **colony of Saint Domingo:** Saint Domingue. The eastern part of the island of Hispaniola was under Spanish control (now the Dominican Republic); the western part (now Haiti) had been under French control before the rebellion.

[Then] Gen. Leclerc[2] came. Why did he not inform me of his powers before landing? Why did he land without my order and in defiance of the order of the Commission? Did he not commit the first hostilities? Did he not seek to gain over the generals and other officers under my command by every possible means? . . .

In regard to the Constitution, the subject of one charge against me: Having driven from the colony the enemies of the Republic, calmed the factions and united all parties; perceiving, after I had taken possession of St. Domingo, that the Government made no laws for the colony, and feeling the necessity of police regulations for the security and tranquility of the people, I called an assembly of wise and learned men, composed of deputies from all the communities, to conduct this business.

When this assembly met, I represented to its members that they had an arduous and responsible task before them; that they were to make laws adapted to the country, advantageous to the Government, and beneficial to all—laws suited to the localities, to the character and customs of the inhabitants.

The Constitution must be submitted for the sanction of the Government, which alone had the right to adopt or reject it. Therefore, as soon as the Constitution was decided upon and its laws fixed, I sent the whole, by a member of the assembly, to the Government to attain sanction. The errors or faults which this Constitution may contain cannot therefore be imputed to me. At the time of Leclerc's arrival, I had heard nothing from the Government upon this subject. Why today do they seek to make a crime of that which is no crime? Why put truth for falsehood, and falsehood for truth? Why put darkness for light and light for darkness? . . .

If Gen. Leclerc went to the colony to do evil, it should not be charged upon me. It is true that only one of us can be blamed; but however little one may wish to do me justice, it is clear that he is the author of all the evils which the island has suffered, since, without warning me, he entered the colony, which he found in a state of prosperity, fell upon the inhabitants, who were at their work, contributing to the welfare of the community, and shed their blood upon their native soil. That is the true source of the evil.

If two children were quarreling together, should not their father or mother stop them, find out which was the aggressor, and punish him, or punish them, if they were both wrong? Gen. Leclerc had no right to arrest me; Government alone could arrest us both, hear us, and judge us. Yet Gen. Leclerc enjoys liberty, and I am in a dungeon.…

Having given an account of my conduct since the arrival of the fleet at St. Domingo, I will enter into some details of previous events.

Since I entered the service of the Republic, I have not claimed a penny of my salary; Gen. Laveaux, Government agents, all responsible persons connected with the public treasury, can do me this justice, that no one has been more prudent, more disinterested than I. I have only now and then received the extra pay allowed me; very often I have not asked even this. Wherever I have taken money from the treasury, it has been for some public use; the governor [*l'ordonnateur*] has used it as the service

---

[2] **Gen. Leclerc:** Charles Victor Emmanuel Leclerc, Pontoise Val-d'Oise (1772–1802), was the general appointed by Napoleon to re-establish French control over St. Domingue. Acting on Napoleon's instructions, Leclerc tricked and seized Toussaint during a meeting and deported him to France, where he died in prison in 1803 after writing the present account.

required. I remember that once only, when far from home, I borrowed six thousand francs from Citizen Smith who was governor of the Department of the South.

I will sum up, in a few words, my conduct and the results of my administration. At the time of the evacuation of the English, there was not a penny in the public treasury; money had to be borrowed to pay the troops and the officers of the Republic. When Gen. Leclerc arrived he found three millions, five hundred thousand francs in the public fund. When I returned to Cayes, after the departure of Gen. Rigaud, the treasury was empty; Gen. Leclerc found three millions there; he found proportionate sums in all the private depositories on the island.

Thus it is seen that I did not serve my country from interested motives; but, on the contrary, I served it with honor, fidelity, and integrity, sustained by the hope of receiving, at some future day, flattering acknowledgements from the government; all who know me will do me this justice.

I have been a slave; I am willing to own it; but I have never received reproaches from my masters.

I have neglected nothing at Saint Domingo for the welfare of the island; I have robbed myself of rest to contribute to it; I have sacrificed everything for it. I have made it my duty and pleasure to develop the resources of this beautiful colony. Zeal, activity, courage—I have employed them all.

The island was invaded by the enemies of the Republic; I had then but a thousand men, armed with pikes. I sent them back to labor in the field, and organized several regiments, by the authority of Gen. Laveaux.

The Spanish portion had joined the English to make war upon the French. Gen. Desfourneaux was sent to attack Saint Michel with well-disciplined troops of the line; he could not take it. General Laveaux ordered me to the attack; I carried it. It is to be remarked that, at the time of the attack by Gen. Desfourneaux, the place was not fortified, and that when I took it, it was fortified by bastions in every corner. I also took Saint-Raphaël and Hinche, and rendered an account to Gen. Laveaux.

The English were entrenched at Pont-de-l'Ester; I drove them from the place. They were in possession of Petite Rivière. Among the posts gained at Petite Rivière, was a fortification defended by seven pieces of canon, which I attacked, and carried by assault. I also conquered the Spaniards entrenched in the camps of Miraut and DuBorg at Verrettes. I gained a famous victory[3] over the English in a battle which lasted from six in the morning until nearly night. This battle was so fierce that the roads were filled with the dead, and rivers of blood were seen on every side.

I took all the baggage and ammunition of the enemy, and a large number of prisoners. I sent the whole to Gen. Laveaux, giving him an account of the engagement. All the posts of the English upon the heights of Saint Marc were taken by me; the walled fortifications in the mountains of Fond-Baptiste and Délices, the camp of Drouët in the Matheaux mountains, which the English regarded as impregnable, the citadels of

---

[3] **famous victory:** During the war that broke out in 1793 between Revolutionary France on the one hand and Spain and Great Britain on the other, Toussaint allied himself with France after the Revolutionary government in Paris had promised freedom to slaves who would join the fight against the foreign invaders. Toussaint's army won seven battles in one week against the British forces in January 1794.

Mirebalais, called the Gibraltar of the island, occupied by eleven hundred men, the celebrated camp of l'Acul-du-Saut, the stone fortifications of Trou-d'Eau, three stories high, those of the camp of Decayette and of Beau-Bien—in short, all the fortifications of the English in this quarter were unable to withstand me, as were those of Neybe, of Saint Jean de la Maguâna, of Las Mathas, of Banique and other places occupied by the Spaniards; all were brought by me under the power of the Republic.

I was also exposed to the greatest dangers; several times I narrowly escaped being made prisoner; I shed my blood for my country; I received a ball in the right hip which remains there still; I received a violent blow on the head from a cannon-ball, which knocked out the greater part of my teeth, and loosened the rest. In short, I received upon different occasions seventeen wounds, whose honorable scars still remain. Gen. Laveaux witnessed many of my engagements; he is too honorable not to do me justice: ask him if I ever hesitated to endanger my life, when the good of my country and the triumph of the Republic required it.

If I were to record the various services which I have rendered the Government, I should need many volumes, and even then should not finish them; and, as a reward for all these services, I have been arbitrarily arrested at St. Domingo, bound, and put on board ship like a criminal, without regard for my rank, without the least consideration. Is this the recompense due my labors? Should my conduct lead me to expect such treatment?

I was once rich. At the time of the revolution, I was worth six hundred and forty-eight thousand francs. I spent it in the service of my country. I purchased but one small estate upon which to establish my wife and family. Today, notwithstanding my disinterestedness, they seek to cover me with opprobrium and infamy; I am made the most unhappy of men; my liberty is taken from me; I am separated from all that I hold dearest in the world,—from a venerable father, a hundred and five years old, who needs my assistance, from a dearly-loved wife, who, I fear, separated from me, cannot endure the afflictions which overwhelm her, and from a cherished family, who made the happiness of my life.

On my arrival in France I wrote to the First Consul and to the Minister of Marine, giving them an account of my situation, and asking their assistance for my family and myself. Undoubtedly, they felt the justice of my request, and gave orders that what I asked should be furnished me. But, instead of this, I have received the old half-worn dress of a soldier, and shoes in the same condition. Did I need this humiliation added to my misfortune?

When I left the ship, I was put into a carriage. I hoped then that I was to be taken before a tribunal to give an account of my conduct, and to be judged. Far from it; without a moment's rest I was taken to a fort on the frontiers of the Republic, and confined in a frightful dungeon.

It is from the depths of this dreary prison that I appeal to the justice and magnanimity of the First Consul. He is too noble and too good a general to turn away from an old soldier, covered with wounds in the service of his country, without giving him the opportunity to justify himself, and to have judgment pronounced upon him.

I ask, then, to be brought before a tribunal or council of war, before which, also, Gen. Leclerc may appear, and that we may both be judged after we have both been heard; equity, reason, law, all assure me that this justice cannot be refused me.

—1803

Simón Bolívar 1783–1830

Born in Caracas, Venezuela, to a family with a long aristocratic lineage originating in Biscay in the Basque country, Simón José Antonio de la Santísima Trinidad Bolívar y Ponte Palacios y Blanco is best known as the towering figure of the Spanish American independence—as "el libertador" of northern South America per se. When studying as a young man, his tutors included Andrés Bello (see below) and Simón Rodríguez, a famous intellectual of the Spanish American Enlightenment whose ideas and educational style heavily influenced Bolívar. Following the death of his parents, in 1799, he went to Spain in order to complete his education; there, he married María Teresa Rodríguez del Toro y Alaysa in 1802. However, soon after Bolívar arrived in America with his new wife, she died of yellow fever, and he never remarried. In 1804, Bolívar traveled to Europe once more, and for a time he was part of Napoleon's retinue. Upon his return to America in 1807, Bolívar became involved in the growing movement that demanded independence from Spain, after the motherland had itself been invaded by France and Napoleon had implemented Joseph Bonaparte as King of Spain and her colonies. After the local patriots had occupied Caracas and had proclaimed independence from Spain in 1810, Bolívar was sent to Britain on a diplomatic mission, and Caracas was re-taken by the Spaniards during his absence. Although Bolívar, upon his return, took command of a patriot army and was able to recapture Caracas in 1813, he had to retreat from Venezuela to New Granada (now Colombia), which was also in open rebellion against Spain. There, he took command of a Colombian force and captured Bogotá in 1814, but then suffered new defeats that forced him to flee to Jamaica. Bolívar returned to South America with a new force that he had gathered in Haiti, taking Angostura (now Ciudad Bolívar) in 1816, and dealing the Spaniards a major defeat in Boyar in 1819, which liberated the territory of Colombia. He then returned to Angostura and led the congress that organized the original republic of Gran Colombia (now Ecuador, Colombia, Panama, and Venezuela) and became its first president on December 17, 1819. Thereafter, Bolívar continued the armed struggle for South American independence, defeating the Spanish army at Carabobo in Venezuela on June 24, 1821, and marching into Ecuador. His army won a decisive victory over the Spaniards at Ayacucho in 1824, which ended Spanish power in South America. Bolívar died from tuberculosis on December 17, 1830. Although he is best known for his feats as a general in the Spanish American war of independence and as one of the main architects of South America's early nation states, he was also a prolific and accomplished writer of political tracts, as well as a poet. Bolívar wrote the following letter during his stay in Jamaica. Probably intended for the Duke of Manchester, governor of the island, it discusses the position of the rebellious territories in South America, their poor preparation for self-government, and the chances for success.

Further Reading Antonio Cussen, *Bello and Bolívar: Poetry and Politics in the Spanish American Revolution* (1992).

From The Jamaica Letter[†]

Kingston, Jamaica, September 6, 1815.

My dear Sir:

I hasten to reply to the letter of the 29th last which you had the honor of sending me and which I received with the greatest satisfaction.

Sensible though I am of the interest you desire to take in the fate of my country, and of your commiseration with her for the tortures she has suffered from the time of her discovery until the present at the hands of her destroyers, the Spaniards, I am no less sensible of the obligation which your solicitous inquiries about the principal objects of American policy place upon me. Thus, I find myself in conflict between the desire to reciprocate your confidence, which honors me, and the difficulty of rewarding it, for lack of documents and books and because of my own limited knowledge of a land so vast, so varied, and so little known as the New World. In my opinion it is impossible to answer the questions that you have so kindly posed. Baron von Humboldt[1] himself, with his encyclopedic theoretical and practical knowledge, could hardly do so properly, because, although some of the facts about America and her development are known, I dare say the better part are shrouded in mystery. Accordingly, only conjectures that are more or less approximate can be made, especially with regard to her future and the true plans of the Americans, inasmuch as our continent has within it potentialities for every facet of development revealed in the history of nations, by reason of its physical characteristics and because of the hazards of war and the uncertainties of politics.

As I feel obligated to give due consideration to your esteemed letter and to the philanthropic intentions prompting it, I am impelled to write you these words, wherein you will certainly not find the brilliant thoughts you seek but rather a candid statement of my ideas.

"Three centuries ago," you say, "began the atrocities committed by the Spaniards on this great hemisphere of Columbus." Our age has rejected these atrocities as mythical, because they appear to be beyond the human capacity for evil. Modern critics would never credit them were it not for the many and frequent documents testifying to these horrible truths. The humane Bishop of Chiapas, that apostle of America, Las Casas,[2] has left to posterity a brief description of these horrors, extracted from the trial records in Sevilla relating to the cases brought against the *conquistadores,* and containing the testimony of every respectable person then in the New World, together with the charges, which the tyrants made against each other. All this is attested by the foremost historians of that time. Every impartial person has admitted the zeal, sincerity, and high character of that friend of humanity, who so

---

[†] Source: Simón Bolívar, "Jamaica Letter" in *El Liberatador: Writings of Simón Bolívar.* Edited by David Bushnell. Oxford University Press, 2003. Copyright © 2003 by Oxford University Press. All rights reserved.
[1] **Baron von Humboldt:** Alexander von Humboldt (1769–1859), a famous German naturalist and explorer.
[2] **Las Casas:** Bartolomé de Las Casas (1484–1566), a sixteenth-century Spanish Dominican monk famous for his defense of the rights of the American Indians.

fervently and so steadfastly denounced to his government and to his contemporaries the most horrible acts of sanguinary frenzy.

With what a feeling of gratitude I read that passage in your letter in which you say to me: "I hope that the success which then followed Spanish arms may now turn in favor of their adversaries, the badly oppressed people of South America." I take this hope as a prediction, if it is justice that determines man's contests. Success will crown our efforts, because the destiny of America has been irrevocably decided; the tie that bound her to Spain has been severed. Only a concept maintained that tie and kept the parts of that immense monarchy together. That which formerly bound them now divides them. The hatred that the Peninsula has inspired in us is greater than the ocean between us. It would be easier to have the two continents meet than to reconcile the spirits of the two countries. The habit of obedience; a community of interest, of understanding, of religion; mutual goodwill; a tender regard for the birthplace and good name of our forefathers; in short, all that gave rise to our hopes, came to us from Spain. As a result there was born principle of affinity that seemed eternal, notwithstanding the misbehavior of our rulers which weakened that sympathy, or, rather, that bond enforced by the domination of their rule. At present the contrary attitude persists: we are threatened with the fear of death, dishonor, and every harm; there is nothing we have not suffered at the hands of that unnatural stepmother—Spain. The veil has been torn asunder. We have already seen the light, and it is not our desire to be thrust back into darkness. The chains have been broken; we have been freed, and now our enemies seek to enslave us anew. For this reason America fights desperately, and seldom has desperation failed to achieve victory.

Because successes have been partial and spasmodic, we must not lose faith. In some regions the Independents triumph, while in others the tyrants have the advantage. What is the end result? Is not the entire New World in motion, armed for defense? We have but to look around us on this hemisphere to witness a simultaneous struggle at every point.

The war-like state of the La Plata River provinces has purged that territory and led their victorious armies to Upper Perú, arousing Arequipa and worrying the royalists in Lima. Nearly one million inhabitants there now enjoy liberty.

The territory of Chile, populated by 800,000 souls, is fighting the enemy who is seeking her subjugation; but to no avail, because those who long ago put an end to the conquests of this enemy, the free and indomitable Araucanians,[2] are their neighbors and compatriots. Their sublime example is proof to those fighting in Chile that a people who love independence will eventually achieve it.

The viceroyalty of Perú, whose population approaches a million and a half inhabitants, without doubt suffers the greatest subjection and is obliged to make the most sacrifices for the royal cause; and, although the thought of cooperating with

---

[2] **Araucanians:** Another name for the Mapuche, a Native American ethnic group inhabiting the southern parts of Chile, famous for their indomitable spirit in resisting Spanish (and before, Inca) attempts at conquest.

that part of America may be vain, the fact remains that it is not tranquil, nor is it capable of restraining the torrent that threatens most of its provinces.

New Granada, which is, so to speak, the heart of America, obeys a general government, save for the territory of Quito which is held only with the greatest difficulty by its enemies, as it is strongly devoted to the country's cause; and the provinces of Panamá and Santa Marta endure, not without suffering, the tyranny of their masters. Two and a half million people inhabit New Granada and are actually defending that territory against the Spanish army under General Morillo, who will probably suffer defeat at the impregnable fortress of Cartagena. But should he take that city, it will be at the price of heavy casualties, and he will then lack sufficient forces to subdue the unrestrained and brave inhabitants of the interior.

With respect to heroic and hapless Venezuela, events there have moved so rapidly and the devastation has been such that it is reduced to frightful desolation and almost absolute indigence, although it was once among the fairest regions that are the pride of America. Its tyrants govern a desert, and they oppress only those unfortunate survivors who, having escaped death, lead a precarious existence. A few women, children, and old men are all that remain. Most of the men have perished rather than be slaves; those who survive continue to fight furiously on the fields and in the inland towns, until they expire or hurl into the sea those who, insatiable in their thirst for blood and crimes, rival those first monsters who wiped out America's primitive race. Nearly a million persons formerly dwelt in Venezuela, and it is no exaggeration to say that one out of four has succumbed either to the land, sword, hunger, plague, flight, or privation, all consequences of the war, save the earthquake.

According to Baron von Humboldt, New Spain, including Guatemala, had 7,800,000 inhabitants in 1808. Since that time, the insurrection, which has shaken virtually all of her provinces, has appreciably reduced that apparently correct figure, for over a million men have perished, as you can see in the report of Mr. Walton, who describes faithfully the bloody crimes committed in that abundant kingdom. There the struggle continues by dint of human and every other type of sacrifice, for the Spaniards spare nothing that might enable them to subdue those who have had the misfortune of being born on this soil, which appears to be destined to flow with the blood of its offspring. In spite of everything, the Mexicans will be free. They have embraced the country's cause, resolved to avenge their forefathers or follow them to the grave. Already they say with Raynal:[3] The time has come at last to repay the Spaniards' torture for torture and to drown that race of annihilators in its own blood or in the sea.

The islands of Puerto Rico and Cuba, with a combined population of perhaps 700,000 to 800,000 souls, are the most tranquil possessions of the Spaniards,

---

[3] **Raynal:** Guillaume Thomas François Raynal (1713–1796), a famous French Enlightenment philosopher and historian of the New World, who was critical of Spanish imperialism.

because they are not within range of contact with the Independents. But are not the people of those islands Americans? Are they not maltreated? Do they not desire a better life?

This picture represents, on a military map, an area of 2,000 longitudinal and 900 latitudinal leagues at its greatest point, wherein 16,000,000 Americans either defend their rights or suffer repression at the hands of Spain, which, although once the world's greatest empire, is now too weak, with what little is left her, to rule the new hemisphere or even to maintain herself in the old. And shall Europe, the civilized, the merchant, the lover of liberty allow an aged serpent, bent only on satisfying its venomous rage, devour the fairest part of our globe? What! Is Europe deaf to the clamor of her own interests? Has she no eyes to see justice? Has she grown so hardened as to become insensible? The more I ponder these questions, the more I am confused. I am led to think that America's disappearance is desired; but this is impossible because all Europe is not Spain. What madness for our enemy to hope to re-conquer America when she has no navy, no funds, and almost no soldiers! Those troops which she has are scarcely adequate to keep her own people in a state of forced obedience and to defend herself from her neighbors. On the other hand, can that nation carry on the exclusive commerce of one-half the world when it lacks manufactures, agricultural products, crafts and sciences, and even a policy? Assume that this mad venture were successful, and further assume that pacification ensued, would not the sons of the Americans of today, together with the sons of the European *reconquistadores* twenty years hence, conceive the same patriotic designs that are now being fought for?

Europe could do Spain a service by dissuading her from her rash obstinacy, thereby at least sparing her the costs she is incurring and the blood she is expending. And if she will fix her attention on her own precincts she can build her prosperity and power upon more solid foundations than doubtful conquests, precarious commerce, and forceful exactions from remote and powerful peoples. Europe herself, as a matter of common sense policy, should have prepared and executed the project of American independence, not alone because the world balance of power so necessitated, but also because this is the legitimate and certain means through which Europe can acquire overseas commercial establishments. A Europe which is not moved by the violent passions of vengeance, ambition, and greed, as is Spain, would seem to be entitled, by all the rules of equity, to make clear to Spain where her best interests lie.

All of the writers who have treated this matter agree on this point. Consequently, we have had reason to hope that the civilized nations would hasten to our aid in order that we might achieve that which must prove to be advantageous to both hemispheres. How vain has been this hope! Not only the Europeans but even our brothers of the North have been apathetic bystanders in this struggle which, by its very essence, is the most just, and in its consequences the most noble and vital of any which have been raised in ancient or in modern times. Indeed, can the far-reaching effects of freedom for the hemisphere which Columbus discovered ever be calculated?

"The criminal action of Bonaparte," you say, "in seizing Charles IV and Ferdinand VII, the monarchs of that nation which three centuries ago treacherously imprisoned two rulers of South America, is a most evident sign of divine retribution, and, at the same time, positive proof that God espouses the just cause of the Americans and will grant them independence."

It appears that you allude to Montezuma, the ruler of Mexico, who was imprisoned by Cortés, and, according to Herrera, was by him slain, although Solís states that it was the work of the people; and to Atahualpa, the Inca of Perú, destroyed by Francisco Pizarro and Diego Almagro. The fate of the monarchs of Spain and of America is too different to admit a comparison. The former were treated with dignity and were kept alive, and eventually they recovered their freedom and their throne; whereas the latter suffered unspeakable tortures and the vilest of treatment. Quauhtemotzin [Guatémoc], Montezuma's successor, was treated as an emperor and crowned, but in ridicule and not in honor, so that he might suffer this humiliation before being put to torture. A like treatment was accorded the ruler of Michoacán, Catzontzin; the *zipa* of Bogotá, and all the other *toquis, imas, zipas, ulmenes, caciques*,[4] and other Indian dignitaries who succumbed before Spain's might.

The case of Ferdinand VII more nearly parallels what happened in Chile in 1535 to the *ulmen* of Copiapó, then ruler of that region. The Spaniard Almagro pretended, like Bonaparte, to espouse the cause of the legitimate sovereign; he therefore called the other a usurper, as did Ferdinand in Spain. Almagro appeared to re-establish the legitimate sovereign in his estates but ended by shackling the hapless *ulmen* and feeding him to the flames without so much as hearing his defense. This is similar to the case of Ferdinand VII and his usurper: Europe's monarchs, however, only suffer exile; the *ulmen* of Chile is barbarously put to death.

"These several months," you add, "I have given much thought to the situation in America and to her hopes for the future. I have a great interest in her development, but I lack adequate information respecting her present state and the aspirations of her people. I greatly desire to know about the politics of each province, also its peoples, and whether they desire a republic or a monarchy; or whether they seek to form one unified republic or a single monarchy? If you could supply me with this information or suggest the sources I might consult, I should deem it a very special favor."

Generous souls always interest themselves in the fate of a people who strive to recover the rights to which the Creator and Nature have entitled them, and one must indeed be wedded to error and passion not to harbor this noble sentiment. You have given thought to my country and are concerned in its behalf, and for your kindness I am warmly grateful.

I have listed the population, which is based on more or less exact data, but which a thousand circumstances render deceiving. This inaccuracy cannot easily be remedied, because most of the inhabitants live in rural areas and are often nomadic; they

---

[4] *toquis, imas, zipas, ulmenes, caciques*: Words for leaders and/or chiefs in various Latin American Indian languages.

are farmers, herders, and migrants, lost amidst thick giant forests, solitary plains, and isolated by lakes and mighty streams. Who is capable of compiling complete statistics of a land like this! Moreover, the tribute paid by the Indians, the punishments of the slaves, the first fruits of the harvest, tithes, and taxes levied on farmers, and other impositions have driven the poor Americans from their homes. This is not to mention the war of extermination that has already taken a toll of nearly an eighth part of the population and frightened another large part away. All in all, the difficulties are insuperable, and the tally is likely to show only half the true count.

It is even more difficult to foresee the future fate of the New World, to set down its political principles, or to prophesy what manner of government it will adopt. Every conjecture relative to America's future is, I feel, pure speculation. When mankind was in its infancy, steeped in uncertainty, ignorance, and error, was it possible to foresee what system it would adopt for its preservation? Who could venture to say that a certain nation would be a republic or a monarchy; this nation great, that nation small? To my way of thinking, such is our own situation. We are a young people. We inhabit a world apart, separated by broad seas. We are young in the ways of almost all the arts and sciences, although, in a certain manner, we are old in the ways of civilized society. I look upon the present state of America as similar to that of Rome after its fall. Each part of Rome adopted a political system conforming to its interest and situation or was led by the individual ambitions of certain chiefs, dynasties, or associations. But this important difference exists: those dispersed parts later reestablished their ancient nations, subject to the changes imposed by circumstances or events. But we scarcely retain a vestige of what once was; we are, moreover, neither Indian nor European, but a species midway between the legitimate proprietors of this country and the Spanish usurpers. In short, though Americans by birth we derive our rights from Europe, and we have to assert these rights against the rights of the natives, and at the same time we must defend ourselves against the invaders. This places us in a most extraordinary and involved situation. Notwithstanding that it is a type of divination to predict the result of the political course which America is pursuing, I shall venture some conjectures which, of course, are colored by my enthusiasm and dictated by rational desires rather than by reasoned calculations.

The role of the inhabitants of the American hemisphere has for centuries been purely passive. Politically they were nonexistent. We are still in a position lower than slavery, and therefore it is more difficult for us to rise to the enjoyment of freedom. Permit me these transgressions in order to establish the issue. States are slaves because of either the nature or the misuse of their constitutions; a people is therefore enslaved when the government, by its nature or its vices, infringes on and usurps the rights of the citizen or subject. Applying these principles, we find that America was denied not only its freedom but even an active and effective tyranny. Let me explain. Under absolutism there are no recognized limits to the exercise of governmental powers. The will of the great sultan, khan, rey, and other despotic rulers is the supreme law, carried out more or less arbitrarily by the lesser pashas, khans, and satraps of Turkey and Persia, who have an organized system of oppression in which inferiors participate according to the authority vested in them. To them is entrusted the administration of civil, military, political, religious, and tax matters. But, after all is said and done, the rulers of Ispahan are Persians; the viziers of the Grand Turk are Turks; and the sultans of Tartary are Tartars. China does not bring its military leaders and scholars from the land of Genghis Khan, her conqueror, notwithstanding that the Chinese of today are the lineal descendants of those who were reduced to subjection by the ancestors of the present-day Tartars.

How different is our situation! We have been harassed by a conduct which has not only deprived us of our rights but has kept us in a sort of permanent infancy with regard to public affairs. If we could at least have managed our domestic affairs and our internal administration, we could have acquainted ourselves with the processes and mechanics of public affairs. We should also have enjoyed a personal consideration, thereby commanding a certain unconscious respect from the people, which is so necessary to preserve amidst revolutions. That is why I say we have even been deprived of an active tyranny, since we have not been permitted to exercise its functions.

Americans today, and perhaps to a greater extent than ever before, who live within the Spanish system occupy a position in society no better than that of serfs destined for labor, or at best they have no more status than that of mere consumers. Yet even this status is surrounded with galling restrictions, such as being forbidden to grow European crops, or to store products which are royal monopolies, or to establish factories of a type the Peninsula itself does not possess. To this add the exclusive trading privileges, even in articles of prime necessity, and the barriers between American provinces, designed to prevent all exchange of trade, traffic, and understanding. In short, do you wish to know what our future held?—simply the cultivation of the fields of indigo, grain, coffee, sugar cane, cacao, and cotton; cattle raising on the broad plains; hunting wild game in the jungles; digging in the earth to mine its gold—but even these limitations could never satisfy the greed of Spain.

So negative was our existence that I can find nothing comparable in any other civilized society, examine as I may the entire history of time and the politics of all nations. Is it not an outrage and a violation of human rights to expect a land so splendidly endowed, so vast, rich, and populous, to remain merely passive?

As I have just explained, we were cut off and, as it were, removed from the world in relation to the science of government and administration of the state. We were never viceroys or governors, save in the rarest of instances; seldom archbishops and bishops; diplomats never; as military men, only subordinates; as nobles, without royal privileges. In brief, we were neither magistrates nor financiers and seldom merchants—all in flagrant contradiction to our institutions.

Emperor Charles V made a pact with the discoverers, conquerors, and settlers of America, and this, as Guerra puts it, is our social contract. The monarchs of Spain made a solemn agreement with them, to be carried out on their own account and at their own risk, expressly prohibiting them from drawing on the royal treasury. In return, they were made the lords of the land, entitled to organize the public administration and act as the court of last appeal, together with many other exemptions and privileges that are too numerous to mention. The King committed himself never to alienate the American provinces, inasmuch as he had no jurisdiction but that of sovereign domain. Thus, for themselves and their descendants, the *conquistadores* possessed what were tantamount to feudal holdings. Yet there are explicit laws respecting employment in civil, ecclesiastical, and tax-raising establishments. These laws favor, almost exclusively, the natives of the country who are of Spanish extraction. Thus, by an outright violation of the laws and the existing agreements, those born in America have been despoiled of their constitutional rights as embodied in the code.

From what I have said it is easy to deduce that America was not prepared to secede from the mother country; this secession was suddenly brought about by the effect of the illegal concessions of Bayonne and the unrighteous war which the Regency unjustly and illegally declared on us. Concerning the nature of the Spanish governments, their stringent and hostile decrees, and their long record of desperate behavior, you can find articles of real merit, by Mr. Blanco, in the newspaper *El Español.* Since this aspect of our history is there very well treated, I shall do no more than refer to it.

The Americans have risen rapidly without previous knowledge of, and, what is more regrettable, without previous experience in public affairs, to enact upon the world stage the eminent roles of legislator, magistrate, minister of the treasury, diplomat, general, and every position of authority, supreme or subordinate, that comprises the hierarchy of a fully organized state.

When the French invasion, stopped only by the walls of Cadiz, routed the fragile governments of the Peninsula, we were left orphans. Prior to that invasion, we had been left to the mercy of a foreign usurper. Thereafter, the justice due us was dangled before our eyes, raising hopes that only came to naught. Finally, uncertain of our destiny, and facing anarchy for want of a legitimate, just, and liberal government, we threw ourselves headlong into the chaos of revolution. Attention was first given to obtaining domestic security against enemies within our midst, and then it was extended to the procuring of external security. Authorities were set up to replace those we had deposed, empowered to direct the course of our revolution and to take full advantage of the fortunate turn of events; thus we were able to found a constitutional government worthy of our century and adequate to our situation.

The first steps of all the new governments are marked by the establishment of *juntas* of the people. These *juntas* speedily draft rules for the calling of congresses, which produce great changes. Venezuela erected a democratic and federal government, after declaring for the rights of man. A system of checks and balances was established, and general laws were passed granting civil liberties, such as freedom of the press and others. In short, an independent government was created. New Granada uniformly followed the political institutions and reforms introduced by Venezuela, taking as the fundamental basis of her constitution the most elaborate federal system ever to be brought into existence. Recently the powers of the chief executive have been increased, and he has been given all the powers that are properly his. I understand that Buenos Aires and Chile have followed this same line of procedure, but, as the distance is so great and documents are so few and the news reports so unreliable, I shall not attempt even briefly to sketch their progress.

Events in Mexico have been too varied, confused, swift, and unhappy to follow clearly the cause of that revolution. We lack, moreover, the necessary documentary information to enable us to form a judgment. The Independents of Mexico, according to our information, began their insurrection in September, 1810, and a year later they erected a central government in Zitacuaro, where a national *junta* was installed under the auspices of Ferdinand VII, in whose name the government was carried on. The events of the war caused this *junta* to move from place to place; and, having undergone such modifications as events have determined, it may still be in existence.

It is reported that a generalissimo or dictator has been appointed and that he is the illustrious General Morelos, though others mention the celebrated General Rayón. It is certain that one or both of these two great men exercise the supreme authority in that country. And recently a constitution has been created as a framework of government. In March, 1812, the government, then residing in Zultepec, submitted a plan for peace and war to the Viceroy of Mexico that had been conceived with the utmost wisdom. It acclaimed the law of nations and established principles that are true and beyond question. The *junta* proposed that the war be fought as between brothers and countrymen; that it need not be more cruel than a war between foreign nations; that the rules of nations and of war, held inviolable even by infidels and barbarians, must be more binding upon Christians, who are, moreover, subject to one sovereign and to the same laws; that prisoners not be treated as guilty of *lèse majesté*,[5] nor those surrendering arms slain, but rather held as hostages for exchange; and that peaceful towns not be put to fire and sword. The *junta* concluded its proposal by warning that if this plan were not accepted rigorous reprisal would be taken. This proposal was received with scorn: no reply was made to the national *junta*. The original communications were publicly burned in the plaza in Mexico City by the executioner, and the Spaniards have continued the war of extermination with their accustomed fury; meanwhile, the Mexicans and the other American nations have refrained from instituting a war to the death respecting Spanish prisoners. Here it can be seen that as a matter of expediency an appearance of allegiance to the King and even to the Constitution of the monarchy has been maintained. The national *junta*, it appears, is absolute in the exercise of the legislative, executive, and judicial powers, and its membership is very limited.

Events in Costa Firme have proved that institutions which are wholly representative are not suited to our character, customs, and present knowledge. In Caracas party spirit arose in the societies, assemblies, and popular elections; these parties led

---

[5] *lèse majesté*: A French expression (from the Latin *Laesa maiestas* or *Laesae maiestatis [crimen]*) for crime or injury to the Majesty.

us back into slavery. Thus, while Venezuela has been the American republic with the most advanced political institutions, she has also been the clearest example of the inefficacy of the democratic and federal system for our new-born states. In New Granada, the large number of excess powers held by the provincial governments and the lack of centralization in the general government have reduced that fair country to her present state. For this reason her foes, though weak, have been able to hold out against all odds. As long as our countrymen do not acquire the abilities and political virtues that distinguish our brothers of the north, wholly popular systems, far from working to our advantage, will, I greatly fear, bring about our downfall. Unfortunately, these traits, to the degree in which they are required, do not appear to be within our reach. On the contrary, we are dominated by the vices that one learns under the rule of a nation like Spain, which has only distinguished itself in ferocity, ambition, vindictiveness, and greed.

It is harder, Montesquieu has written, to release a nation from servitude than to enslave a free nation. This truth is proven by the annals of all times, which reveal that most free nations have been put under the yoke, but very few enslaved nations have recovered their liberty. Despite the convictions of history, South Americans have made efforts to obtain liberal, even perfect, institutions, doubtless out of that instinct to aspire to the greatest possible happiness, which, common to all men, is bound to follow in civil societies founded on the principles of justice, liberty, and equality. But are we capable of maintaining in proper balance the difficult charge of a republic? Is it conceivable that a newly emancipated people can soar to the heights of liberty, and, unlike Icarus,[6] neither have its wings melt nor fall into an abyss? Such a marvel is inconceivable and without precedent. There is no reasonable probability to bolster our hopes.

More than anyone, I desire to see America fashioned into the greatest nation in the world, greatest not so much by virtue of her area and wealth as by her freedom and glory. Although I seek perfection for the government of my country, I cannot persuade myself that the New World can, at the moment, be organized as a great republic. Since it is impossible, I dare not desire it; yet much less do I desire to have all America a monarchy because this plan is not only impracticable but also impossible. Wrongs now existing could not be righted, and our emancipation would be fruitless. The American states need the care of paternal governments to heal the sores and wounds of despotism and war. The parent country, for example, might be Mexico, the only country fitted for the position by her intrinsic strength, and without such power there can be no parent country. Let us assume it were to be the Isthmus of Panamá, the most central point of this vast continent. Would not all parts continue in their lethargy and even in their present disorder? For a single government to infuse life into the New World; to put into use all the resources for public prosperity; to improve, educate, and perfect the New World, that government

---

[6] **Icarus:** In Greek mythology, the son of the artificer Daedalus who fell to his death into the Icarian Sea when he flew too close to the sun, which melted the wax holding his artificial wings together.

would have to possess the authority of a god, much less the knowledge and virtues of mankind.

The party spirit that today keeps our states in constant agitation would assume still greater proportions were a central power established, for that power—the only force capable of checking this agitation—would be elsewhere. Furthermore, the chief figures of the capitals would not tolerate the preponderance of leaders at the metropolis, for they would regard these leaders as so many tyrants. Their resentments would attain such heights that they would compare the latter to the hated Spaniards. Any such monarchy would be a misshapen colossus that would collapse of its own weight at the slightest disturbance.

Mr. de Pradt has wisely divided America into fifteen or seventeen mutually independent states, governed by as many monarchs. I am in agreement on the first suggestion, as America can well tolerate seventeen nations; as to the second, though it could easily be achieved, it would serve no purpose. Consequently, I do not favor American monarchies. My reasons are these: The well-understood interest of a republic is limited to the matter of its preservation, prosperity, and glory. Republicans, because they do not desire powers which represent a directly contrary viewpoint, have no reason for expanding the boundaries of their nation to the detriment of their own resources, solely for the purpose of having their neighbors share a liberal constitution. They would not acquire rights or secure any advantage by conquering their neighbors, unless they were to make them colonies, conquered territory, or allies, after the example of Rome. But such thought and action are directly contrary to the principles of justice which characterize republican systems; and, what is more, they are in direct opposition to the interests of their citizens, because a state, too large of itself or together with its dependencies, ultimately falls into decay. Its free government becomes a tyranny. The principles that should preserve the government are disregarded, and finally it degenerates into despotism. The distinctive feature of small republics is permanence: that of large republics varies, but always with a tendency toward empire. Almost all small republics have had long lives. Among the larger republics, only Rome lasted for several centuries, for its capital was a republic. The rest of her dominions were governed by given laws and institutions.

The policy of a king is very different. His constant desire is to increase his possessions, wealth, and authority; and with justification, for his power grows with every acquisition, both with respect to his neighbors and his own vassals, who fear him because his power is as formidable as his empire, which he maintains by war and conquest. For these reasons I think that the Americans, being anxious for peace, science, art, commerce, and agriculture, would prefer republics to kingdoms. And, further, it seems to me that these desires conform with the aims of Europe.

We know little about the opinions prevailing in Buenos Aires, Chile, and Perú. Judging by what seeps through and by conjecture, Buenos Aires will have a central government in which the military, as a result of its internal dissensions and external wars, will have the upper hand. Such a constitutional system will necessarily degenerate into an oligarchy or a monocracy, with a variety of restrictions the exact nature of which no one can now foresee. It would be unfortunate if this situation were to follow because the people there deserve a more glorious destiny.

The Kingdom of Chile is destined, by the nature of its location, by the simple and virtuous character of its people, and by the example of its neighbors, the proud republicans of Arauco, to enjoy the blessings that flow from the just and gentle laws of a republic. If any American republic is to have a long life, I am inclined to believe it will be Chile. There the spirit of liberty has never been extinguished; the vices of Europe and Asia arrived too late or not at all to corrupt the customs of that distant corner of the world. Its area is limited; and, as it is remote from other peoples, it will always remain free from contamination. Chile will not alter her laws, ways, and practices. She will preserve her uniform political and religious views. In a word, it is possible for Chile to be free.

Perú, on the contrary, contains two factors that clash with every just and liberal principle: gold and slaves. The former corrupts everything; the latter are themselves corrupt. The soul of a serf can seldom really appreciate true freedom. Either he loses his head in uprisings or his self-respect in chains. Although these remarks would be applicable to all America, I believe that they apply with greater justice to Lima, for the reasons I have given and because of the cooperation she has rendered her masters against her own brothers, those illustrious sons of Quito, Chile, and Buenos Aires. It is plain that he who aspires to obtain liberty will at least attempt to secure it. I imagine that in Lima the rich will not tolerate democracy, nor will the freed slaves and *pardos*[7] accept aristocracy. The former will prefer the tyranny of a single man, to avoid the tumult of rebellion and to provide, at least, a peaceful system. If Perú intends to recover her independence, she has much to do.

From the foregoing, we can draw these conclusions: The American provinces are fighting for their freedom, and they will ultimately succeed. Some provinces as a matter of course will form federal and some central republics; the larger areas will inevitably establish monarchies, some of which will fare so badly that they will disintegrate in either present or future revolutions. To consolidate a great monarchy will be no easy task, but it will be utterly impossible to consolidate a great republic.

It is a grandiose idea to think of consolidating the New World into a single nation, united by pacts into a single bond. It is reasoned that, as these parts have a common origin, language, customs, and religion, they ought to have a single government to permit the newly formed states to unite in a confederation. But this is not possible. Actually, America is separated by climatic differences, geographic diversity, conflicting interests, and dissimilar characteristics. How beautiful it would be if the Isthmus of Panamá could be for us what the Isthmus of Corinth was for the Greeks! Would to God that some day we may have the good fortune to convene there an august assembly of representatives of republics, kingdoms, and empires to deliberate upon the high interests of peace and war with the nations of the other three-quarters of the globe. This type of organization may come to pass in some happier period of our regeneration. But any other plan, such as that of Abbé St. Pierre, who in laudable

---

[7] *pardos*: Racially mixed or "brown" people.

delirium conceived the idea of assembling a European congress to decide the fate and interests of those nations, would be meaningless.

Among the popular and representative systems, I do not favor the federal system. It is over-perfect, and it demands political virtues and talents far superior to our own. For the same reason I reject a monarchy that is part aristocracy and part democracy, although with such a government England has achieved much fortune and splendor. Since it is not possible for us to select the most perfect and complete form of government, let us avoid falling into demagogic anarchy or monocratic tyranny. These opposite extremes would only wreck us on similar reefs of misfortune and dishonor; hence, we must seek a mean between them. I say: Do not adopt the best system of government, but the one that is most likely to succeed.

By the nature of their geographic location, wealth, population, and character, I expect that the Mexicans, at the outset, intend to establish a representative republic in which the executive will have great powers. These will be concentrated in one person, who, if he discharges his duties with wisdom and justice, should almost certainly maintain his authority for life. If through incompetence or violence he should excite a popular revolt and it should be successful, this same executive power would then, perhaps, be distributed among the members of an assembly. If the dominant party is military or aristocratic, it will probably demand a monarchy that would be limited and constitutional at the outset, and would later inevitably degenerate into an absolute monarchy; for it must be admitted that there is nothing more difficult in the political world than the maintenance of a limited monarchy. Moreover, it must also be agreed that only a people as patriotic as the English are capable of controlling the authority of a king and of sustaining the spirit of liberty under the rule of sceptre and crown.

The states of the Isthmus of Panamá as far as Guatemala, will perhaps form a confederation. Because of their magnificent position between two mighty oceans, they may in time become the emporium of the world. Their canals will shorten distances throughout the world, strengthen commercial ties between Europe, America, and Asia, and bring to that happy area tribute from the four quarters of the globe. There some day, perhaps, the capital of the world may be located—reminiscent of the Emperor Constantine's claim that Byzantium was the capital of the ancient world.

New Granada will unite with Venezuela, if they can agree to the establishment of a central republic. Their capital may be Maracaibo or a new city to be named Las Casas (in honor of that humane hero) to be built on the borders of the two countries, in the excellent port area of Bahía-Honda. This location, though little known, is the most advantageous in all respects. It is readily accessible, and its situation is so strategic that it can be made impregnable. It has a fine, healthful climate, a soil as suitable for agriculture as for cattle raising, and a superabundance of good timber. The Indians living there can be civilized, and our territorial possessions could be increased with the acquisition of the Goajira Peninsula. This nation should be called Colombia as a just and grateful tribute to the discoverer of our hemisphere. Its government might follow the English pattern, except that in place of a king there will be an executive who will be elected, at most, for life, but his office will never be hereditary, if a republic is desired. There will be a hereditary legislative chamber or senate. This body can interpose itself between the violent demands of the people and the great powers of the government during periods of political unrest. The second representative body will be a legislature with restrictions no greater than those of the lower house in England. The Constitution will draw on all systems of government, but I do not want it to partake of all their vices. As Colombia is my country, I have an indisputable right to desire for her that form of government which, in my opinion, is best. It is very possible that New Granada may not care to recognize a central government, because she is greatly addicted to federalism; in such event, she will form a separate state which, if it endures, may prosper, because of its great and varied resources.

"Great and beneficial changes," you say, "can frequently be brought about through the efforts of individuals." The South Americans have a tradition to this effect: When Quetzalcoatl,[8] the Hermes or Buddha of South America, gave up his ministry and left his people, he promised them he would return at an ordained time to re-establish his government and revive their prosperity. Does not this tradition foster a conviction that he may shortly reappear? Can you imagine the result if an individual were to appear among these people, bearing the features of Quetzalcoatl, their Buddha of the forest, or those of Mercury, of whom other nations have spoken? Do you suppose that this would affect all regions of America? Is it not unity alone that is needed to enable them to expel the Spaniards, their troops, and the supporters of corrupt Spain and to establish in these regions a powerful empire with a free government and benevolent laws?

Like you, I believe that the specific actions of individuals can produce general results, especially in revolutions. But is that hero, that great prophet or God of Anáhuac,[9] Quetzalcoatl, capable of effecting the prodigious changes that you propose? This esteemed figure is not well known, if at all, by the Mexican people: such is the fate of the defeated, even if they be gods. Historians and writers, it is true, have undertaken a careful investigation of his origin, the truth or falsity of his doctrine, his prophesies, and the account of his departure from Mexico. Whether he was an apostle of Christ or a pagan is openly debated. Some would associate his name with St. Thomas;[10] others, with the Feathered Serpent; while still others say he is the famous prophet of Yucatán, Chilan-Cambal. In a word, most Mexican authors, polemicists, and secular historians have discussed, at greater or lesser length, the question of the true character of Quetzalcoatl. The fact is, according to the historian, Father Acosta,[11] that he established a religion which, in its rites, dogmas, and mysteries, bore a remarkable similarity to the religion of Jesus, the faith that it probably most resembles. Nevertheless, many Catholic writers have tried to dismiss the idea that he was a true

---

[8] **Quetzalcoatl:** In pre-Columbian meso-American religion, the Plumed-Serpent god and Lord of Tula, who had departed to the west, leaving a prophecy of his return.

[9] **Anáhuac:** An ancient name for a Mesoamerican, particularly Mexica (Aztec), area or areas roughly indentical with the Valley of Mexico.

[10] **St. Thomas:** Judas Thomas Didymus (?-ca. 72), one of the twelve apostles of Jesus Christ; he is believed to have worked as an apostle of the Christian faith in India and died near Madras. Several sixteenth- and seventeenth-

century historians claimed that he had also arrived and worked in the New World, leaving signs of Christianity there later found by Spanish missionaries. Some of these early modern historians claimed an identity between St. Thomas and Quetzalcoatl, the Meso-American god.

[11] **Father Acosta:** José de Acosta (1539–1600), a Spanish Jesuit and one of the most important sixteenth-century historians of the New World.

prophet, and they refuse to associate him with St. Thomas, as other celebrated writers have done. The general opinion is that Quetzalcoatl was a divine law-giver among the pagan peoples of Anáhuac that their great Montezuma was his lieutenant, deriving his power from that divinity. Hence it may be inferred that our Mexicans would not follow the pagan Quetzalcoatl, however ingratiating the guise in which he might appear, for they profess the most intolerant and exclusive of all religions.

Happily, the leaders of the Mexican independence movement have made use of this fanaticism to excellent purpose by proclaiming the famous Virgin of Guadalupe the Queen of the Patriots, invoking her name in all difficult situations and placing her image on their banners. As a result, political enthusiasms have been commingled with religion, thus producing an intense devotion to the sacred cause of liberty. The veneration of this image in Mexico is greater than the exaltation that the most sagacious prophet could inspire.

Surely unity is what we need to complete our work of regeneration. The division among us, nevertheless, is nothing extraordinary, for it is characteristic of civil wars to form two parties, conservatives and reformers. The former are commonly the more numerous, because the weight of habit induces obedience to established powers; the latter are always fewer in number although more vocal and learned. Thus, the physical mass of the one is counterbalanced by the moral force of the other; the contest is prolonged, and the results are uncertain. Fortunately, in our case, the mass has followed the learned.

I shall tell you with what we must provide ourselves in order to expel the Spaniards and to found a free government. It is *union*, obviously; but such union will come about through sensible planning and well-directed actions rather than by divine magic. America stands together because it is abandoned by all other nations. It is isolated in the center of the world. It has no diplomatic relations, nor does it receive any military assistance; instead, America is attacked by Spain, which has more military supplies than any we can possibly acquire through furtive means.

When success is not assured, when the state is weak, and when results are distantly seen, all men hesitate; opinion is divided, passions rage, and the enemy fans these passions in order to win an easy victory because of them. As soon as we are strong and under the guidance of a liberal nation which will lend us her protection, we will achieve accord in cultivating the virtues and talents that lead to glory. Then will we march majestically toward that great prosperity for which South America is destined. Then will those sciences and arts which, born in the East, have enlightened Europe, wing their way to a free Colombia, which will cordially bid them welcome.

Such, Sir, are the thoughts and observations that I have the honor to submit to you, so that you may accept or reject them according to their merit. I beg you to understand that I have expounded them because I do not wish to appear discourteous and not because I consider myself competent to enlighten you concerning these matters.
I am, Sir, etc., etc.

Simón Bolívar

—1815

Andrés Bello 1781–1865

Andrés Bello was born in Caracas, Venezuela, in 1781, and studied classics, philosophy, and medicine at the University of Caracas. He became known early on for his translations of Horace and was recognized in literary circles as a gifted neoclassical poet. In 1799, he met the German naturalist Alexander von Humboldt, who was visiting Venezuela during his scientific expedition through South America and who strengthened Bello's interest in the natural sciences. One of Bello's early poetic productions, an ode entitled "A la vacuna," celebrated the introduction of vaccination in Venezuela. He also worked as an educator, with students as prominent as Simón Bolívar. Upon the emergence of the Spanish American independence movements in 1810, he was sent, along with Bolívar, to London in order to enlist the support of Great Britain in the war for independence from Spain. Although the delegation secured only a commitment to neutrality from Great Britain, Bello remained in London for nineteen years, working as a tutor, translator, and journalist. After the end of the Revolutionary War, Bello worked for the Legations of Chile and Colombia. Meanwhile, his various intellectual activities included the production of editions of medieval French and Spanish epic poetry; studies, with James Mills, of Jeremy Bentham's modern economic theories; and the publication of periodicals such as *El Censor Americano* (1820), *La Biblioteca Americana* (1823), and *El Repertorio Americano* (1826–1827). Some of Bello's most important poems were published in these journals, including "Alocución a la poesía" (Allocution to Poetry) (1823) and the poem excerpted here, "La Agricultura de la zona tórrida" (Agriculture in the Torrid Zone) (1826), all of which were concerned with America's cultural, intellectual, and literary autonomy. For this reason, Bello has been compared to his contemporary in the United States, Ralph Waldo Emerson. In 1829, Bello followed an invitation of the Chilean government to come to Santiago and take charge of Chile's national organ, *El Araucano*—a post that also entailed an appointment as Subsecretary in the Ministry of Foreign Affairs. Thus, Bello became a Chilean citizen and spent the rest of his life in Santiago, where he founded the University of Chile, wrote Chile's civil code, and authored numerous works on international law, philosophy, literature, and linguistics.

Further Reading Antonio Cussen, *Bello and Bolívar: Poetry and Politics in the Spanish American Revolution* (1992).

From Agriculture in the Torrid Zone[†]

Hail to thee, fertile zone,–
Where the enamored sun in daily round
Enfolds thee, where beneath thy kisses shows
All that each various climate grows,
Brought forth from out thy ground!–
In spring thou bindst her garlands of the ears
Of richest corn; thou giv'st the grape
Unto the sopping case; no form nor shape
Of purple, red or yellow flower appears

5

[†] Source: *Hispanic Anthology*, collected, arranged, and translated by Thomas Walsh (New York: G. P. Putnam's Sons, 1920).

10   Unknown to thy soft bowers;
     The odors of thy thousand flowers
     The wind's delight afford;
     Across thy pasture sward
     The countless flocks go grazing from the plain
15   Whose only boundary the horizon sets,
     Unto the surging mountains, where
     Lifting the snows into the inaccessible air
     They hold their parapets.
     Thou givest, too, the beauty of the cane
20   Where honey sweet is stored
     That leaves the beehive in disdain;
     Thou in thy coral urns bring'st forth the bean
     Which soon in chocolate in the cup is poured;
     With blaze of scarlet are thy nopals[1] seen
25   Such as the Tyrian sea-shell[2] never knew;
     Thy plant of indigo such hues afford
     As ne'er from out the sapphire's heart looked through
     Thine is the wine the pierced agave stores
     To glad Anahuac's joyous sons; and thine
30   The fragrant leaf whose gentle steaming pours
     With solace when their hearts a weary pine.
     Thy jasmines clothe the Arab brush,
     Whose perfumes rare the savage rage refine
     And cool the Bacchic[3] flush;
35   And for the children of thy land
     The stately palm-tree's fronds are far displayed
     And the ambrosial pineapple's shade.
     The yucca-tree holds forth its snowy breads;
     And ruddy glow the broad potato beds;
40   The cotton bush to greet the lightest airs
     Its rose of gold and snowy fleece prepares.
     ....
     Within thy hand the passiflower blooms
     In branches of far-showing green
     And thy sarmentum's twining fronds afford
45   Nectarean globes and stripéd flowers' perfumes.
     For thee the maize, the haughty lord
     Of all thy ripened harvests, high is seen;
     For thee the rich banana's heavy tree
     Displays its sweetest store –

---

[1] **nopals:** A vegetable made from the young stem segments of the prickly pear.
[2] **Tyrian sea-shell:** A marine snail known as *Murex brandaris* or the Spiny dye-murex with a hypobranchial gland secreting a mucus from which is procured Tyrian purple, also known as *royal purple* or *imperial purple*, a purple-red dye made by the ancient Canaanites/Phoenicians in the city of Tyre.
[3] **Bacchic:** Pertaining to Bacchus, the Greek god of wine and revelry.

50   The proud banana, richest treasury
That Providence in bounteousness could pour
With gracious hand on Ecuador!
It asks no human culture for its aid,
Ere its first fruits are displayed,
55   Nor with the pruning-knife nor plough it shares
The honorable harvest that it bears.
Not even the slightest care it needs
Of pious hands about it shed,
And to its ripeness so it speeds
60   That hardly is it harvested,
Ere a new crop is ripened in its stead.

....

Oh, youngest of the nations, lift your brow
Crowned with new laurels in the marveling West!
Give honor to the fields, the simple life endow,
65   And hold the plains and modest farmer blest!
So that among you evermore shall reign
Fair Liberty enshrined,
Ambition modified, and Law composed,
Thy people's paths immortal there to find
70   Not fickle nor in vain!–
So emulous Time shall see disclosed
New generations and new names of might,
Blazing in highest light
Beside your heroes old!
75   "These are my sons! Behold!"–
(You shall declare amain)–
Sons of the fathers who did climb
The Andes' peaks in years agone,–
Of those who great Boyaca's sands upon,–
80   In Maipu and in Junin sublime,–
On Apurima's[4] glorious plain,
Did triumph o'er the lion of old Spain.

—1826

José María Heredia (1803–1839)

Born in Santiago de Cuba and permanently exiled as a young man, Heredia has been called the earliest great Cuban poet, the first to develop a poetics of anti-colonial independence and to inscribe a proto-national Cuban ideal in his Romantic verses. But Heredia was also a major figure in the U.S. Hispanophone publishing world—a transnational and often revolutionary community of journalists and belle-lettristes—from the time of his arrival in 1823 until long after his early death. Over the course of his

---

[4] **Boyaca ... Apurima:** Famous battle sites in the Spanish American wars for independence.

short life, Heredia worked as a poet, editor, publisher, translator, dramatist, essayist, and political analyst, addressing the problems of love and revolution, indigenous history and classical philosophy, politics and civic duty, exile and loss. As a young student, Heredia met the Cuban reformist and future literary leader, Domingo del Monte, and joined a secret society called Los Soles y Rayos de Bolívar (The Suns and Rays of Bolivar)—a group named for the famous South American liberator, and known for advocating Cuban independence from Spanish rule. Charged with conspiracy against Spanish authorities in 1823, Heredia fled to the United States, where his first collection of poetry, *Poesías de José María Heredia*, was published in 1825. Among his most well-known verses, soon read throughout Latin America, were "En un teocalli de Cholula" (In a Temple of Cholula); "A Emilia" (To Emilia); "Al huracán" (To the Hurricane); "La Estrella de Cuba" (The Star of Cuba); and "Himno del desterrado" (The Exile's Song). Heredia composed "Niágara" in 1824, on a visit to Niagara Falls; the poem was translated as "Ode to Niagara" into English in 1827 by William Cullen Bryant, who called it "the best which has been written about the Great American Cataract." But "Niágara" was more than a celebration of the poet's inspiration before the sublime beauty and terror of the Falls; it was also a meditation on the personal and political crisis of a Cuban exile—one who would return to the land of his birth only briefly, in 1836, after having recanted on the political ideal of an independent Cuba in order to obtain permission to visit his mother, whom he had not seen for more than a decade. For this, his former revolutionary compatriots would not forgive him; branded as a traitor to the cause of freedom, Heredia returned to Mexico, where he died within three years. A half century later, however, his poetic and political reputation found new life in the speeches and writings of the Cuban poet and revolutionary, José Martí, who famously defined Heredia not only as a great Cuban poet but as "el primer poeta de América"—"the first poet of America"—in the full hemispheric sense of the word.

Further Reading Kirsten Silva Gruesz, *Ambassadors of Culture: The Transamerican Origins of Latino Writing* (2002), esp. "The Cuban Star Over New York," pp. 39–48; José María Heredia, *Niágara y otros textos: Poesía y prosa selectas*, ed. Angel Augier Caracas (1990).

—*Anna Brickhouse, University of Virginia*

Ode to Niagara[†]

My lyre! give me my lyre! My bosom feels
The glow of inspiration. O how long
Have I been left in darkness since this light
Last visited my brow, Niagara!
5 Thou with thy rushing waters dost restore
The heavenly gift that sorrow took away.
Tremendous torrent! for an instant hush
The terrors of thy voice and cast aside
Those wide involving shadows, that my eyes

[†] Source: José María Heredia, "Ode to Niagara" in *The Odes of Bello, Olmedo, and Heredia*, ed. and trans. Elijah Clarence Hills (New York: G. P. Putnam's Sons, 1920).

10 May see the fearful beauty of thy face!
I am not all unworthy of thy sight,
For from my very boyhood have I loved,
Shunning the meaner track of common minds,
To look on nature in her loftier moods.

15 At the fierce rushing of the hurricane,
At the near bursting of the thunderbolt,
I have been touched with joy; and when the sea
Lashed by the wind, hath rocked my bark and showed
Its yawning caves beneath me, I have loved
20 Its dangers and the wrath of elements.
But never yet the madness of the sea
Hath moved me as thy grandeur moves me now.

Thou flowest on in quiet, till thy waves
Grow broken 'midst the rocks; thy current then
25 Shoots onward like the irresistible course
Of destiny. Ah, terribly they rage–
The hoarse and rapid whirlpools there!
My brain grows wild, my senses wander, as I gaze
Upon the hurrying waters, and my sight
30 Vainly would follow, as toward the verge
Sweeps the wide torrent–waves innumerable
Meet there and madden–waves innumerable
Urge on and overtake the waves before,
And disappear in thunder and foam

35 They reach–they leap the barrier–the abyss
Swallows insatiable the sinking waves.
A thousand rainbows arch them, and woods
Are deafened with the roar. The violent shock
Shatters to vapor the descending sheets–
40 A cloudy whirlwind fills the gulf, and heaves
The mighty pyramid of circling mist
To heaven. The solitary hunter near
Pauses with terror in the forest shades.
What seeks thy restless eye? Why are not here,
45 About the jaws of this abyss the palms.
Ah, the delicious palms—that on the plains
of my own native Cuba spring and spread
Their thickly foliaged summits to the sun,
And, in the breathings of the ocean air,
50 Wave soft beneath the heaven's unspotted blue?

But no, Niagara,–thy forest pines
Are fitter coronal for thee. The palm,

The effeminate myrtle and frail rose may grow
In gardens, arid give out their fragrance there,
55 Unmanning him who breathes it. Thine it is
To do a nobler office. Generous minds
Behold thee, and are moved, and learn to rise
Above earth's frivolous pleasures; they partake
Thy grandeur, at the utterance of thy name.
60 God of all truth! in other lands I've seen
Lying philosophers, blaspheming Men,
Questioners of thy mysteries, that draw
Their fellows deep into impiety;
And therefore doth my spirit seek thy face
65 In earth's majestic solitudes. Even here
My heart doth open all itself to thee.
In this immensity of loneliness
I feel thy hand upon me. To my ear
The eternal thunder of the cataract brings
70 Thy voice, and I am humbled as I hear.

Dread torrent! that with wonder and with fear
Dost overwhelm the soul of him that looks
Upon thee, and dost bear it from itself,
Whence hast thou thy beginning? Who supplies,
75 Age after age, thy unexhausted springs?
What power hath ordered, that, when all thy weight
Descends into the deep, the swollen waves
Rise not, and roll to overwhelm the earth?
The Lord hath opened his omnipotent hand,
80 Covered thy face with clouds, and given his voice
To thy down-rushing waters; he hath girt
Thy terrible forehead with his radiant bow.
I see thy never-resting waters run
And I bethink me how the tide of time
85 Sweeps to eternity. So pass of man–
Pass, like a noon-day dream–the blossoming days,
And he awakes to sorrow. I, alas!
Feel that my youth is withered, and my brow
Plowed early with the lines of grief and care.

90 Never have I so deeply felt as now
The hopeless solitude, the abandonment,
The anguish of a loveless life. Alas!
How can the impassioned, the unfrozen heart
Be happy without love? I would that one
95 Beautiful,–worthy to be loved and joined
In love with me,–now shared my lonely walk

On this tremendous brink. 'Twere sweet to see
Her sweet face touched with paleness, and become
More beautiful from fear, and overspread
100   With a faint smile, while clinging to my side!
Dreams–dreams! I am an exile, and for me
There is no country and there is no love.
Hear, dread Niagara, my latest voice!
Yet a few years, and the cold earth shall close
105   Over the bones of him who sings thee now
Thus feelingly. Would that this, my humble verse,
Might be like thee, immortal! I, meanwhile,
Cheerfully passing to the appointed rest,
Might raise my radiant forehead in the clouds
110   To listen to the echoes of my fame.

—1824

Juan Francisco Manzano (1797–1854)

Juan Francisco Manzano was born an urban slave in 1797, in Havana, Cuba. Having taught himself to read and write at an early age, he came to the attention of a number of prominent Cuban intellectuals, most notably Domingo del Monte, who was a Venezuelan by birth and who had married one of the richest women in Cuba. Encouraged by this group, Manzano first published his *Poesías líricas* in 1821, then *Flores pasajeras* in 1830, both in Havana. Also upon the encouragement of del Monte and his circle, in 1837, he wrote his autobiography, which was circulated by del Monte and reached a British officer in charge of the prosecution of the violators of the slave trade in the Caribbean by the name of Richard Madden. It was Madden who was responsible for the first publication of Manzano's autobiography, which he had translated into English (along with some of Manzano's poetry) and published in London in 1840. After del Monte bought Manzano out of slavery for five hundred pesos, Manzano wrote one more work, a play entitled *Zafira* (1842). In 1844, Manzano became entangled in charges relating to a conspiracy plot to overthrow the colonial regime, which resulted in his imprisonment and the execution of another famous early Afro-Cuban poet— Gabriel de la Concepción Valdés, better known as Plácido. Manzano's mentor, del Monte, also became implicated in the plot and had to leave Cuba, dying in exile in Spain in 1853. Although Manzano was able to prove his innocence and was released from prison, he died a year after del Monte, in 1854. His autobiography was not published in its original Spanish until 1936, when it appeared in Madrid.

Further Reading Alma Dizon, "Mothers, Morals, and Power in the Autobiography of Juan Francisco Manzano," *Revista de Estudios Hispánicos (Puerto Rico)*, 21 (1994): 109–117; Luis A. Jiménez, "Nineteenth Century Autobiography in the Afro-Americas: Frederick Douglass and Juan Francisco Manzano," *Afro-Hispanic Review*, 14.2 (Fall 1995): 47–52.

From The Autobiography of a Cuban Slave[†]

THE Senora Donna Beatrice, the wife of Don Juan M—— took a pleasure every time she went to her beautiful estate, the Molino, to make choice of the finest Creole children about the age of ten or eleven years, and carry them to town, where she gave them instruction conformable to their new condition. Her house was always filled with these young slaves instructed in everything necessary to her service. One of the favourite young slaves was Maria M——, my mother, who was greatly esteemed for her intelligence, and her occupation was to wait on the Senora Marquesa of J. in her advanced age. This lady was accustomed when she was pleased with her attendants, to give them their liberty when they were about to marry, if it were with some mechanic likewise free; providing them with all things necessary, as if they had been her own children, without depriving them after their marriage of the favour and protection of her house, which extended even to their children and husbands; of which conduct there are many notable examples, amongst those who were not even born in the house. Various changes, however, taking place in the service, Maria became the chief waiting-woman of the Marquesa. In this situation she married Toribio de Castro, and in due time, I was ushered into the world.

My master took a fancy to me, and it is said I was more in his arms than in those of my mother. She had all the privileges of a slave who had acted as a dry-nurse, and also partly as a wet-nurse, *media criandera;*[1] and having married one of the head slaves of the house, and given a little Creole to her mistress, I was called by this lady, "the child of her old age," I was brought up by the side of my mistress without separating from her, except at bed-time, and she never went out without taking me in her *volante*.[2] With the difference of hours in respect to some, and days in regard to others, I was the contemporary of Don Miguel de C., and also of Don Manuel O'R. now Count of B.; which two families lived in a splendid house, close to the Machina, separated only by doors which divided the apartments; for, in fact, it was two houses made into one.

It would be tedious to detail the particulars of my childhood, treated by my mistress with greater kindness than I deserved, and whom I was accustomed to call "my mother." At six years of age, on account, perhaps, of too much vivacity, more than anything else, I was sent to school to my godmother every day at noon; and every evening I was brought to the house, that my mistress might see me, who seldom went out without seeing me, for if she did, I roared and cried, and so disturbed the house, that sometimes it was necessary to send for the whip, which nobody dared to lay on me, for not even my parents were authorised to flog me, and I knowing this, often took advantage of it. On one occasion, being very bold, my father beat me, but my mistress hearing of it, did not allow him for many days to come into her pres-

---

[†] Source: *Poems by a Slave in the Island of Cuba, Recently Liberated; Translated from the Spanish, by R. R. Madden, M.D. With the History of the Early Life of the Negro Poet, Written by Himself; to Which Are Prefixed Two Pieces Descriptive of Cuban Slavery and the Slave-Traffic, by R. R. M.* (London: Thomas Ward and Co., 1840).

[1] *media criandera*: This term is applied to a negress who at the same time suckles her own infant, and that of her mistress [Madden's note].

[2] *volante*: The helm of the carriage.

ence, until he procured the intercession of her Confessor, the father Maya, a Franciscan, and then he was forgiven; after the latter had explained to him that my Senora, as mistress, and my father, as a parent, had each their respective direction of me.

At ten years of age, I learned by heart some of the longest sermons of Father Louis, of Grenada, and the visitors who came to the house on Sundays, used to hear me repeat them when I came from the chapel, where I was sent with my godmother, to learn how to behave in church; because, although the service was performed every Sunday in the house, I was not permitted to be present, on account of the tricks I might have played with the other children.

I also knew my catechism well, and as much of religion as a woman could teach me. I knew how to sew tolerably, and to place the furniture in order. On one occasion, I was taken to the Opera, and received some presents for reciting what I heard, but many more for the sermons, and my parents got what I received in the drawing-room.

But passing over much of my early history, in which there was nothing but happiness, I must not omit the circumstances which happened at my baptism; on that occasion, I was dressed in the same robe in which the Senora Donna Beatrice was baptized, which was celebrated with great rejoicings, my father being skilled in music, and playing on the flute and clarionet; and my mistress desiring to solemnize that day with one of her noble traits of generosity, in part liberated my parents by "coartacion," giving them the power at any time of purchasing their liberty at the sum of three hundred dollars each; what greater happiness could be looked for at her hands.

At the age of ten, I was placed under the care of my godfather; having learned something of my father's trade, which was that of a tailor, previously, to being sent to the estate. My mother gave birth to two other children. One of them, for what reason I know not, was made free—and this one died. My father lamenting his death, saying, "if things had been otherwise, I might have been content, my two living children are slaves, and the one that was free is dead"; whereupon my generous mistress had a document prepared, in which it was declared that the next child they should have should be free; and it happened that twins were subsequently born, who are still living, and both were freed. My parents now were removed to the estate of the Molino, where they were placed in charge of the house, and about this period the Marquesa died there. I was sent for in her last illness. I remember little of what happened on my arrival, except being at the bed-side of my mistress with my mother, Donna Joaquina, and the priest, and that her hand rested on my shoulder, while my mother and Donna Joaquina wept a great deal, and spoke about something which I did not understand, and then that I was taken away. Soon after I went to play, and the following morning I saw her stretched on a large bed, and cried, and was carried down stairs where the other servants were mourning for their mistress; and all night long all the negroes of the estate made great lamentation, repeated the rosary, and I wept with them.

I was taken to the Havana, to my godfather, with whom I soon learned my mistress had left me; for some years I saw nothing of my father. My godfather had taken up his residence in the court-yard of the Count, in the street *Inquisidor*, where I was accustomed to go about the house, and to leave it when I thought proper, without knowing whether I had a master or not.

But one day, being permitted to go to the house of the Marquesa, to see my old acquaintances there, I know not what passed there, but when I was about returning to my godfather, and my dear godmother, I was not allowed to go: here I was clothed in a rich livery, with a great deal of gold lace, and what with my fine clothes, going to the theatres, to *tertulias*,[3] balls, and places of amusement, I soon forgot my old quiet mode of life, and the kindness even of my godmother herself. After some time I was taken to the house of Donna Joaquina, who treated me like a white child, saw that I was properly clothed, and even combed my hair herself; and as in the time of the Marquesa de J., she allowed me not to pray with the other negro children at church— and at mealtime my plate was given to me to eat at the feet of the Senora Marquesa de P., and all this time I was far away from my father and mother.

I had already at the age of twelve years composed some verses in memory, be- cause my godfather did not wish me to learn to write, but I dictated my verses by stealth to a young mulatto girl, of the name of Serafina, which verses were of an amatory character. From this age, I passed on without many changes in my lot to my fourteenth year; but the important part of my history began when I was about eigh- teen, when fortune's bitterest enmity was turned on me, as we shall see hereafter.

For the slightest crime of boyhood, it was the custom to shut me up in a place for charcoal, for four-and-twenty hours at a time. I was timid in the extreme, and my prison, which still may be seen, was so obscure, that at mid-day no object could be dis- tinguished in it without a candle. Here after being flogged I was placed, with orders to the slaves, under threats of the greatest punishment, to abstain from giving me a drop of water. What I suffered from hunger and thirst, tormented with fear, in a place so dismal and distant from the house, and almost suffocated with the vapours arising from the common sink, that was close to my dungeon, and constantly terrified by the rats that passed over me and about me, may be easily imagined. My head was filled with frightful fancies, with all the monstrous tales I had ever heard of ghosts and apparitions, and sorcery; and often when a troop of rats would arouse me with their noise, I would imagine I was surrounded by evil spirits, and I would roar aloud and pray for mercy; and then I would be taken out and almost flayed alive, again shut up, and the key taken away, and kept in the room of my mistress, the Senora herself. On two occasions, the Senor Don Nicholas and his brother showed me compassion, introducing through an aperture in the door, a morsel of bread and some water, with the aid of a coffee-pot with a long spout. This kind of punishment was so frequent that there was not a week that I did not suffer it twice or thrice, and in the country on the estate I suffered a like martyr- dom. I attribute the smallness of my stature and the debility of my constitution to the life of suffering I led, from my thirteenth or fourteenth year.

My ordinary crimes were—not to hear the first time I was called; or if at the time of getting a buffet, I uttered a word of complaint; and I led a life of so much misery, daily receiving blows on the face, that often made the blood spout from both my nostrils; no sooner would I hear myself called than I would begin to shiver, so

---

[3] **tertulias**: A social gathering with literary or artistic overtones.

that I could hardly keep on my legs, but supposing this to be only shamming on my part, frequently would I receive from a stout negro lashes in abundance.

About the age of fifteen or sixteen, I was taken to Matanzas once more, and embraced my parents and brothers.

The character, grave, and honourable of my father, and being always in his sight, caused my time to pass a little lighter than before. I did not suffer the horrible and continual scourgings, nor the blows of the hand, that an unfortunate boy is wont to suffer far away from his miserable parents; notwithstanding, my unfortunate cheeks were slapped often enough. We passed five years in Matanzas; where my employment was to sweep and clean the house as well as I could at sunrise, before any one in the house was up; this done I had to seat myself at the door of my mistress, that she might find me there when she awoke, then I had to follow her about wherever she went, like an automaton with my arms crossed. When breakfast, or the other meals were over, I had to gather up what was left, and having to put my hand to clear away the dishes, and when they rose from table I had to walk behind them. Then came the hour of sewing. I had to seat myself in sight of my mistress to sew women's dresses, to make gowns, shifts, robes, pillow-cases, to mark and to hem fine things in cambric, and mend all kinds of clothing.

At the hour of drawing, which a master taught, I was also present, stationed behind a chair, and what I saw done and heard, corrected and explained, put me in the condition of counting myself as one of the pupils of the drawing-class. One of the children, I forget which, gave me an old tablet, and a crayon; and with my face turned to the wall, the next day I sat down in a corner, and began making mouths, eyes, ears, and going on in this way, I came to perfect myself, so that I was able to copy a head so faithfully, that having finished one, my mistress observing me, showed it to the master, who said that I would turn out a great artist, and that it would be for her one day a great satisfaction that I should take the portraits of all my masters.

At night I had to go to sleep at twelve or one o'clock, some ten or twelve squares of buildings distant, where my mother lived (in the negro *barracones*[4]). Being extremely timid, it was a serious matter to me to pass to this place in the wettest nights. With these troubles, and other treatment something worse, my character became every day more grave and melancholy, and my only comfort was to fly to the arms of my mother, for my father was of a sterner nature. He used to be sleeping when my poor mother and my brother Florence waited up for me, till the hour of my arrival.

Some attacks of ague, which nearly ended my days, prevented me from accompanying my mistress to Havana. When I recovered, no one could enjoy himself in two years as I did in four months; I bathed four times a day, and even in the night. I fished, rode on horseback, made excursions into the mountains, ascended the highest hills, ate all kinds of fruits; in short, I enjoyed all the innocent pleasures of youth. In this little epoch I grew stout and lively, but when I returned to my old mode of life, my health broke down again, and I became as I was before.

---

[4] *barracones*: Living quarters.

When I recovered sufficiently, my first destiny was to be a page, as well in Havana as in Matanzas; already I was used to sit up from my earliest years the greatest part of the night, in the city, either at the theatre, or at parties, or in the house of the Marquis M——H—— and the Senoras C., from which we went out at ten o'clock, and after supper play began, and continued till eleven or twelve; and at Matanzas, on the days appointed, and sometimes not, when they dined at the house of the Count J., or in that of Don Juan M., and generally to pass the evening in the house of the Senoras G., in which the most distinguished persons of the town met and played at *trecillo*, *malilla*, or *burro*. While my lady played, I could not quit the side of her chair till midnight, when we usually returned to the Molino. If during the *tertullia* I fell asleep, or when behind the *volante*, if the lanthorn went out by accident, even as soon as we arrived, the mayoral, or administrador was called up, and I was put for the night in the stocks, and at day-break I was called to an account, not as a boy; and so much power has sleep over a man, four or five nights seldom passed that I did not fall into the same faults. My poor mother and brothers more than twice sat up waiting for me while I was in confinement, waiting a sorrowful morning.

She, all anxiety when I did not come, used sometimes to leave her hut, and approaching the door of the infirmary, which was in front of the place allotted to the men where the stocks were, on the left hand side, at times would find me there; and would call to me, "Juan," and I sighing, would answer her, and then she would say outside, "Ah, my child!" and then it was she would call on her husband in his grave—for at this time my father was dead.

Three times I remember the repetition of this scene; at other times I used to meet my mother seeking me—once above all, a memorable time to me—when the event which follows happened:—

We were returning from the town late one night, when the *volante* was going very fast, and I was seated as usual, with one hand holding the bar, and having the lanthorn in the other, I fell asleep, and it fell out of my hand; on awaking, I missed the lanthorn, and jumped down to get it, but such was my terror, I was unable to come up with the *volante*. I followed, well knowing what was to come, but when I came close to the house, I was seized by Don Sylvester, the young mayoral. Leading me to the stocks, we met my mother, who giving way to the impulses of her heart, came up to complete my misfortunes. On seeing me, she attempted to inquire what I had done, but the mayoral ordered her to be silent, and treated her as one raising a disturbance. Without regard to her entreaties, and being irritated at being called up at that hour, he raised his hand, and struck my mother with the whip. I felt the blow in my own heart! To utter a loud cry, and from a downcast boy, with the timidity of one as meek as a lamb, to become all at once like a raging lion, was a thing of a moment—with all my strength I fell on him with teeth and hands, and it may be imagined how many cuffs, kicks, and blows were given in the struggle that ensued.

My mother and myself were carried off and shut up in the same place; the two twin children were brought to her, while Florence and Fernando were left weeping alone in the hut. Scarcely it dawned, when the mayoral, with two negroes acting under him, took hold of me and my mother, and led us as victims to the place of sacrifice. I suffered more punishment than was ordered, in consequence of my attack on the mayoral. But who can describe the powers of the laws of nature on mothers? The fault of my mother was, that seeing they were going to kill me, as she thought, she inquired what I had done, and this was sufficient to receive a blow and to be further chastised. At beholding my mother in this situation, for the first time in her life (she being exempted from work), stripped by the negroes and thrown down to be scourged, overwhelmed with grief and trembling, I asked them to have pity on her for God's sake; but at the sound of the first lash, infuriated like a tiger, I flew at the mayoral, and was near losing my life in his hands; but let us throw a veil over the rest of this doleful scene.

I said before, that I was like my mistress's lap-dog, since it was my duty to follow her wherever she went, except to her own private rooms, for then I remained outside to prevent any body from going in, receiving any messages, and keeping silence when she was there. One afternoon, I followed her into the garden, where I was set to gather up flowers and transplant some little roots, when the gardener was employed in his occupation there. At the time of leaving the garden, I took unconsciously, a small leaf, one alone of geranium, thinking only of making verses; I was following, with this little leaf in my hand, two or three yards behind my mistress, so absent in my mind that I was squeezing the leaf with my fingers to give it greater fragrancy. At the entrance of the ante-chamber she turned back, I made room for her, but the smell attracted her attention; full of anger, on a sudden and in a quick tone she asked me, "What have you got in your hands?" Motionless and trembling, I dropt the remains of the leaf, and, as if it was a whole plant, for this crime I was struck on the face, and delivered to the care of the overseer, Don Lucas Rodriguez. It was about six o'clock in the afternoon, and in the middle of winter. The *volante* was ready to go to town, and I was to ride behind; but alas! I was little aware what was to come in the next hour! Instead of riding in the *volante*, I was taken to the stocks, which were in a building, formerly an infirmary, and now used for a prison, and for depositing the bodies of the dead till the hour of interment. My feet were put in the stocks, where shivering with cold, without any covering, they shut me in. What a frightful night I passed there! My fancy saw the dead rising and walking about the room, and scrambling up to a window above the river and near a cataract, I listened to its roar, which seemed to me like the howling of a legion of ghosts. Scarcely day-light appeared, when I heard the unbolting of the door; a negro came in followed by the overseer wrapt in his cloak; they took me out and put me on a board fixed on a kind of fork, where I saw a bundle of rods. The overseer, from under a handkerchief over his mouth, roared out, "tie him fast"; when my hands were tied behind like a criminal, and my feet secured in an aperture of the board. Oh, my God! Let me not speak of this frightful scene! When I recovered I found myself in the arms of my mother, bathed in tears, and disconsolate, who, at the request of Don Jaime Florido, left me and retired. When my mistress rose next morning, her first care was to inquire whether I was treated as I deserved; and the servant who was waiting on her called me; and she asked, if I would dare to take any more leaves of her geranium? As I could not answer, I was near undergoing the same punishment, but thought to say, no. About eleven o'clock, I became dangerously ill: three days I was in this state. My mother used to come to see me in the night-time, when she thought my mistress out. At the sixth day I was out of danger, and could walk about. I met my mother one day, who said to me, "Juan, I have got the money to purchase your liberty; as your father is dead, you must act as a father to your brothers; they shall not chastise you any more." My only answer was a flood of tears; she went away, and I to my business; but the result of my mother's visit was disappointment; the money was not paid, and I daily expected the time of my liberty, but that time was not destined for many a long year to come.

Some time after, it happened that a carrier brought to the house some chickens, some capons, and a letter, and as I was always on guard like a sentinel, it was my misfortune to receive them; leaving the fowls outside, I took in the letter to my mistress, who after reading it, ordered me to take them to Don Juan Mato their steward, to whom I delivered what I received. Two weeks after this, I was called to an account for one capon missing, I said without hesitating, that I received three capons, and two chickens, which I delivered. Nothing more was said of the matter, but the following day I saw the mayoral coming along towards the house, who after talking with my mistress for some time, went away again. I served the breakfast, and when I was going to take the first morsel, taking advantage of the moment to eat something, my mistress ordered me to go to the mayoral's house, and tell him—I do not remember what. With sad forebodings, and an oppressed heart, being accustomed to deliver myself up on such occasions, away I went trembling. When I arrived at the door, I saw the mayoral of the Molino, and the mayoral of the Ingenio, together. I delivered my message to the first, who said, "Come in man," I obeyed, and was going to repeat it again, when Senor Dominguez, the mayoral of the Ingenio, took hold of my arm, saying, "it is to me, to whom you are sent"; took out of his pocket a thin rope, tied my hands behind me as a criminal, mounted his horse, and commanded me to run quick before him, to avoid either my mother or my brothers seeing me. Scarcely had I run a mile before the horse, stumbling at every step, when two dogs that were following us, fell upon me; one taking hold of the left side of my face pierced it through; and the other lacerated my left thigh and leg in a shocking manner, which wounds are open yet, notwithstanding it happened twenty-four years ago. The mayoral alighted on the moment, and separated me from their grasp, but my blood flowed profusely, particularly from my leg—he then pulled me by the rope, making use at the same time, of the most disgusting language; this pull partly dislocated my right arm, which at times pains me yet. Getting up, I walked as well as I could, till we arrived at the Ingenio. They put a rope round my neck, bound up my wounds, and put me in the stocks. At night, all the people of the estate were assembled together and arranged in a line, I was put in the middle of them, the mayoral and six negroes surrounded me, and at the word "upon him," they threw me down; two of them held my hands, two my legs, and the other sat upon my back. They then asked me about the missing capon, and I did not know what to say. Twenty-five lashes were laid on me, they then asked me again to tell the truth. I was perplexed; at last, thinking to escape further punishment, I said, "I stole it." "What have you done with the money?" was the next question, and this was another trying point. "I bought a hat." "Where is it?" "I bought a pair of shoes." "No such thing," and I said so many things to escape punishment, but all to no purpose. Nine successive nights the same scene was repeated, and every night I told a thousand lies. After the whipping, I was sent to look after the cattle and work in the fields. Every morning my mistress was informed of what I said the previous night.

At the end of ten days, the cause of my punishment being known, Dionisio Copandonga, who was the carrier who brought the fowls, went to the mayoral, and said that the missed capon was eaten by the steward Don Manuel Pipa, and which capon was left behind in a mistake; the cook Simona was examined and confirmed the account. I do not know whether my mistress was made acquainted with this transaction; but certain it is, that since that moment, my punishment ceased, my fetters were taken off, and my work eased, and a coarse linen dress was put on me. But the same day an accident happened, which contributed much towards my mistress forgiving me.

After helping to load sugar, I was sent to pile blocks of wood in one of the buildings, while so employed, all of a sudden the roof with a loud crash gave way, burying under its ruins the negro Andres Criollo; I escaped unhurt through a back door. The alarm given, all the people came to the rescue of poor Andres, who with great difficulty and labour was taken from under the ruins, with his skull broken, and he died in the Molino a few hours after. Early next morning, as I was piling the refuse of sugar canes, there arrived then Master Pancho, and now Don F., followed by my second brother, who was in his service, and who intimated to me that his master was coming to take me back to the house. This was owing to my brother, who hearing of the accident and my narrow escape, begged earnestly of his young master to intercede with his mother on my behalf, which he easily obtained. I was presented to my mistress, who for the first time received me with kindness. But my heart was so oppressed, that neither her kindness nor eating, nor drinking could comfort me; I had no comfort except in weeping: my mistress observing it, and to prevent my crying so much, and the same time being so very drowsy, ordered me to move about, and clean all the furniture, tables, chairs, drawers, & c. All my liveliness disappeared, and as my brother was greatly attached to me, he became melancholy himself; he tried, however, to cheer me up, but always finished our conversations in tears: for this reason, also, my mistress would not let me wait upon her, nor ride in the *volante* to town; and at last appointed me to the service of young Master Pancho; they bought me a hat and a pair of shoes, a new thing for me, and my master allowed me to bathe, to take a walk in the afternoon, and to go fishing, and hunting with Senor.

Besides the events just related, there happened two other circumstances resembling each other; one while at Havana, and the other at Matanzas, and which I think worth relating, before I begin to speak of my passing to the service of Don Nicolas de C. on my return to Havana. The first of these events happened when the new coin of our C. M. King Ferdinand the Seventh, began to circulate. Don Nicolas gave me a peseta of the old coin one night; next morning there came at the door a beggar, my mistress gave me a peseta of the new coin for him, which calling my attention, and having the other in my pocket, one is as much worth as the other, muttered I to my-self, and changing the pesetas, I gave to the beggar the old one; after I went to my usual place in the antichamber, I sat down in the corner, and taking the new coin out of my pocket, began like a monkey turning it over and over again, when escaping through my fingers it fell down on the floor, making a rattling noise; at its sound my mistress came out of her chamber, made me pick it up; she looked at it, and her face reddened, she bid me go into her chamber, sit in a corner, and wait there; of course, my peseta remained in her possession, she recognised it as the same she gave me for the beggar two minutes before; with such proofs my fate was decided. My mistress was busy going in and out, till at last she sat down to write; soon after the carrier of the Ingenio, who happened to be there at the time with his drove of mules, came into the chamber with a bundle containing a coarse hemp dress, and while he was un-folding it, he dropt a new rope, drawing near me at the same time; trembling, and suspecting his intentions, I sprang up of a sudden, and escaping through another door, ran for protection to Don Nicolas; in the way, I met the young lady Concha, who kindly said to me, "go to my papa." The Marquis was always very kind to me, I used to sleep in his room, and whenever he was afflicted with headache, I gave him warm water, held his head and attended on him till he recovered. When I arrived at his room, which was in an instant, and he saw me at his feet, "What have you done now?" said he; in my confusion I related my case so confusedly, that he understand-ing that I stole the peseta, said in an angry tone, "You knave, why did you steal the peseta?" "No, sir," I replied, "your son Nicolasito gave it to me." "When?" "Last night," said I: we then went to the Senorito's room, who looking at the peseta, said that he did not give it to me. In truth, I was so frightened and confused, that I could not state the particulars sufficiently clear, on account of the presence of the carrier; and the name of the Ingenio, with its new mayoral, Don Simon Diaz, so inspired me with horror, that all conspired to confuse a boy of sixteen years only as I was. The Marquis interceded for me, and for all that, I was shut up in a dungeon four whole days, with-out any food, except what my brother could introduce through a little opening at the bottom of the door, and that was little. At the fifth day I was taken out, dressed with a coarse linen dress and tied with a rope. They were going to send me with the bag-gage of the family, and the other servants, my brother among them, to Matanzas: when the hour arrived, and they were leading me away, I met at the door Donna Beatriz, at present a nun in the Convent of the Ursulinas who interceded for me, that the rope might be taken off, which was done; we embarked in a schooner for Matan-zas, where we arrived at the end of two days.

While on board, and before coming on shore, I changed the coarse dress for the one my brother, unseen, had provided for me; as soon as we landed, my brother and I instead of going with the rest of the servants to present ourselves to Don Juan Go-mez, who had instructions about us from the family, but being ignorant of it, and desirous to see our mother, we left the rest of the servants, and went to the Molino, where after presenting ourselves to the mayoral, and telling him that the rest of the servants were coming, we ran at full speed towards my mother's house; but we scarcely arrived and had time to embrace her, when the Creole, Santiago, greatly agitated and full of anger, called me out, saying, "come with me," not suspecting the secret instructions he had, I refused to go with him, and my mother asking me what have I done, but without giving me time to explain myself, very abruptly took hold of my arm, tied me with a rope, and led me towards the Ingenio Saint Miguel, where we arrived about eleven o'clock, fasting all this time. The mayoral read the letter sent to him from Havana, and then put me in fetters; twenty-five lashes in the morning and as many more in the evening for the term of nine days, was the order of the letter. The mayoral questioned me about the peseta, I told him plainly and truly the fact, and for the first time, this savage man showed pity; he did not put in execution his orders, but sent me to work with the rest of the negroes; here I remained two weeks, when my mistress again sent for me.

The second event happened at Matanzas. My mistress sent me to get change of a gold doubloon at Don Juan de Torres, when I returned, she told me to put the change on a card-table, some time after she took it and put it into her pocket. As it was my business to dust all the furniture every half-hour, whether it was dusty or not, when I came to this card-table, and put down one-half of it, down fell a peseta, which it seems got between the joints; at the sound of it she came from the next room, and asked me about it, I told her how it came there, she then counted her change, and missed the peseta, which she took without saying a word the rest of the day; but next day about ten o'clock, the mayoral of the Ingenio came, who fastened my arms behind me, and ordered me to go before his horse; telling me, at the same time, that my mistress suspected that I put the peseta myself between the joints of the table on purpose to keep it. This mayoral, whose name I do not remember, stopped before a tavern, dismounted, went in, and ordered breakfast for both; untied my arms, and kindly told me to make myself easy and not be afraid. While I was eating, he was conversing with a man, and I heard him say, "his father besought of him to pity me, he had some children of his own." After breakfast he mounted his horse, and made me ride behind him on the horse. When we arrived at the Ingenio, he invited me to dine with him, and at night put me under the care of an old negro woman; I remained in this way nine days, when I was sent for by my mistress. At the period I speak of my father was then living, and used to question me about these things, and advising me to tell always the truth, and to be honest and faithful. As this was the first time that I had been at the Ingenio, and considering the good treatment I experienced, I think it was owing to my mistress's secret instructions.

The second time that I was at Matanzas, there never passed a day without bringing some trouble to me; no, I cannot relate the incredible hardships of my life, a life full of sorrows! My heart sickened through sufferings, once after having received many blows on the face, and that happened almost daily; my mistress said, "I will make an end of you before you are of age"; these words left such an impression on my mind, that I asked my mother the meaning of them, who quite astonished, and after making me repeat them twice over, said, "my son, God is more powerful than the devil." She said no more about it; but this and some hints I received from the old servants of the house, began to unfold the true meaning of her expressions. On another occasion, going to be chastised, for I do not remember what trifle, a gentleman, always kind to me, interceded for me; but my mistress said to him, "mind, Senor, this boy will be one day worse than Rousseau and Voltaire, remember my words." These strange names, and the way that my mistress expressed herself made me very anxious to know what sort of bad people they were; but when I found out, that they were enemies of God, I became more uneasy, for since my infancy I was taught to love and fear God, and my trust in him was such, that I employed always part of the night praying God to lighten my sufferings, and to preserve me from mischief on the following day, and if I did anything wrong I attributed it to my lukewarmness in prayers, or that I might have forgotten to pray; and I firmly believe that my prayers were heard, and to this I attribute the preservation of my life once, on occasion of my running away from Matanzas to Havana, as I will relate hereafter.

Although oppressed with so many sufferings, sometimes I gave way to the impulses of my naturally cheerful character. Whenever I went to Senor Estorino's house, I used to draw decorations on paper, figures on cards or pasteboard, and scenes from Chinese shades, then making frames of wild canes, for puppet shows, with a penknife, the puppets seemed to dance by themselves. I painted also portraits of the sons of Don Felix Llano, Don Manuel and Don Felixe Puebla, Don Francisco Madruga, and many others; to see all this, there used to come several boys of the town, and on these occasions, I used to do my best to enliven these entertainments.

Some time after this, we went to Havana, where I was appointed to the service of young Don Nicolas, who esteemed me not as a slave, but as a son, notwithstanding his youth. In his company the sadness of my soul began to disappear, but soon after I contracted a disease in my chest with a spasmodic cough, of which with the assistance of Doctor Francisco Lubian, and with time and youth, I was perfectly cured. As I said before, I was now kindly treated, and never was without money in my pocket. My business was to take care of his wardrobe, to clean his shoes, and wait upon him: he only forbad me going out by myself, to go to the kitchen, and to have any intercourse with loose characters; and as he himself though young, was very circumspect, so he wished every body about him to be; I never received any reprimand from him, and I loved him very much. As soon as day dawned, I used to get up, prepare his table, arm-chair and books, and I adapted myself so well to his customs, and manners that I began to give myself up to study. From his book of rhetoric I learnt by heart a lesson every day, which I used to recite like a parrot, without knowing the meaning; but being tired of it, I determined to do something more useful, and that was to learn to write: but here was a difficulty, I did not know how to begin, nor did I know how to mend a pen, and I would not touch any of my master's; however, I bought ink, pens, and penknife, and some very fine paper; then taking some of the bits of written paper thrown away by my master, I put a piece of them between one of my fine sheets, and traced the characters underneath, in order to accustom my hand to make letters; with this stratagem, at the end of a month I could write almost the same hand as my master's. Extremely pleased with myself, I employed the hours from five to ten every evening, exercising my hand to write, and in day-time I used to copy the inscriptions at the bottom of pictures hung in the walls; by these means, I could imitate the best hand-writing. My master was told how I employed the evenings, and once he surprised me with all my writing apparatus, but he only advised me to drop that pastime, as not adapted to my situation in life, and that it would be more useful to me to employ my time in needle-work, a business that indeed at the same time I did not neglect. In vain was I forbidden to write, for when everybody went to bed, I used to light a piece of candle, and then at my leisure I copied the best verses, thinking that if I could imitate these, I would become a poet. Once, some of my sonnets fell into one of my friend's hands, and Doctor Coronado was the first to foretell that I would be a great poet, notwithstanding all opposition; he was told how I had taught myself to write, and he encouraged me, saying, that many of the great poets began in the same way.

At this time my master was near contracting an alliance with Senorita Donna Teresa de H., and I was the messenger between them, an office very productive, since I had plenty of money given to me, so much that I did not know what to do with it; I bought a handsome inkstand, a rule, and a good provision of pens, ink, and paper; the rest of my money I sent to my mother. We went to Guanajay on a visit to Count de G., where my future young mistress resided. As the first needle-work my mistress made was dress-making, under the care of Senora Domingo, her dressmaker; I learned to make fine dresses, and I had the honour to make some dresses for my future mistress, in recompense for which I experienced all sorts of kindness; and when they were married I was their page, and as I was so punctual in my attendance on them, I was treated more kindly from day to day. But this happiness lasted only about three years, when my former mistress of Matanzas, hearing reports so favourable of me, resolved to take me into her own service again. At this time I was so punctual in attending sick people, though only eighteen years old, that whenever there was a person ill in the family, they asked permission of my mistress to let me attend upon them. One of them was Don Jose Maria P. who was very ill; I prepared for him his bath, administered the doctor's prescriptions in due time, helped him to rise from his bed, watched the whole of the night, with paper and ink before me, and put down, for the guidance of the doctor, the time that he slept, whether composedly or not, how many times he awoke, how many he coughed, if he snored & c.; I was much praised for this by the doctors, Don Andres Terriltes, Don Nicolas Gutierres, and others. While I was attending this gentleman, my former mistress arrived, and intimated very kindly to me her intention to take me back. I listened to her sorrowfully, for my heart became oppressed at the thoughts of returning to those places so memorable and so sad to me. I was obliged to follow her to her sister's, the Countess of B. where she was on a visit for a few days; she forbade me to bid farewell to my young masters, but I stole away unperceived, and went to take leave of them. Don Nicolas, who since his childhood was very partial to me, took leave of me weeping, as also his lady, both loading me with presents; the Senora gave me some Holland handkerchiefs and two gold doubloons; Don Nicolas all my clothes, including two new coats, and a gold doubloon besides. I left them so downcast and with such sad forebodings, that early next morning I ventured to ask paper and ink, in order to advertise for a new master. This quite astonished my mistress, and saying that she took me back for my own sake, and that I had better stop with her till she made some other arrangements, and when she turned her back I was sorry for having given her this uneasiness. At dinner-time, she mentioned my boldness to her sister the Countess, and, with an angry tone, said to me before all the company, "this is the return you intend to make for all the care I took in your education; did I ever put my hands on you?" I was very near saying, yes, many a time, but thought better to say, no. She then asked me if I remembered her mamma? and at my answering, yes; she said, "I occupy her place, mind that," here the conversation dropt. After prayers in the afternoon, I was sent for by the Countess and Donna Maria Pizarro, who both tried to persuade me to desist from my intention. I plainly told them, that I was afraid of my mistress's fiery temper; this conversation ended by the Countess advising me to stop with my mistress till she thought proper to give me my liberty. Some time after this we left for Matanzas, stopping at the Molino. Here they pointed out to me my new duties, and I acquitted myself so much to their satisfaction, that in a short time I was the head servant of the house. During all this time, after superintending the business of the house, and after breakfast, I used to employ myself at needle-work. At the end of about two weeks after we were in town, it happened that one morning oversleeping myself, a cock found his way into my room, which was close to that of my mistress; the cock crew, I do not know how many times, I only heard him once, I started from my bed, and went about my business, and were it not for the interference of Don Tomas Gener, who, at my request, kindly interceded for me, I should not have escaped being sent to the Molino.

When I was about nineteen years of age, I had some pride in acquitting myself of my duties, so much to the satisfaction of my mistress, and never waited to be ordered twice; at this time I could not bear to be scolded for trifles; but the propensity to humble the self-love of those who are in the good graces of their masters, is contagious disease in all rich families. Such was the case with a person, who without any cause or provocation on my part, began to treat me badly, calling me bad names, all of which I suffered, till he called my mother out of her name: then I retorted on him a similar expression, he gave me a blow, which I could not avoid, and I returned it. My mistress was out, and I was to go after her at the house of the Senora. When we returned, she was told of what happened; I excused myself, saying, that I could not suffer my mother to be called so bad a name; "So," said she, "if he repeats it again, you will not respect my house?" At the third day we went to breakfast to the Molino: meanwhile I was uneasy, I had before me all the vicissitudes of my life, and was apprehensive of what was to come. Soon after our arrival, I saw the mayoral coming towards the house; I escaped through the garden, and hid myself: in the afternoon I went to town, to the Count of G., who gave me shelter and protection; I was still uneasy, I wept bitterly when I remembered the kindness I was treated with by the other masters in Havana. Scarcely was I there five days, when for a trifling fault they sent for a commissary of police, who secured me with a rope, and took me to the public prison in the middle of the day; at four o'clock, there came a white man from the country, who demanded me, and I was delivered to him; he put on me the coarse linen dress, he tied my arms with a rope, and led me towards the Molino, which I desired never to see again, after having been so well treated by my former masters, being now also somewhat elated with the praises bestowed on my abilities, and a little proud of my acquaintance in the city with persons that knew how to reward services. At the Molino, Don Saturnino Carrias, the mayoral at this time, examined me, I told the truth, and he sent me to work at the fields without any chastisement or fetters. I was there about nine days, when my mistress coming to the Molino to breakfast, sent for me, gave me a fine suit of clothes, and took me to town again in the *volante*. I was known at this time under the name of the Chinito, or the little Mulatto of the Marquesa.

About this time I went to the house of the lady of Senor Apodaca, a grandee of Havana, where they were making some preparations for his reception. Senor Apari-cio, a painter and decorator, was employed in painting some emblems allusive to a rose, as the name of the lady was Rosa; I helped the painter, and he gave me ten dol-lars for my work, and having by way of amusement painted some garlands, he saw that I might be useful to him, and asked my mistress to lend me to him, but she would not consent; at the conclusion of his work he gave me two dollars more, which money I kept with the intention to spend it at Havana. My mistress found out that the servants met together in a barn after midnight, to play at cards till the morn-ing. The first thing she did on the following morning was to search my pockets, and finding that I had more money than she gave me, took me for an accomplice in their game; and notwithstanding my telling her how I came in possession of the money, she kept it, and sent me to the Molino, where I was received by the mayoral, and treated kindly, the same as before; at the end of three or four days my mistress sent for me, and I returned to town.

Some time past on without any novelty, when my mother died suddenly. I was made acquainted with this accident soon afterwards, when my mistress gave me three dollars to have prayers said for her. A few days after she gave me leave to go to the Molino, to see what my mother had left. The mayoral gave me the key of the house, where I only found a very large old box empty: as there was a secret in it, which I knew, I pulled the spring, and found there some trinkets of pure gold, but the most worthy were three ancient bracelets, near two inches broad and very thick, two strings of beads, one of gold, the other coral and gold: I found also a bundle of papers, in which were some accounts of debts due to us, one of 200 and odd dollars, another of 400, payable by my mistress, and some others for small sums. When I was born, my grandfather gave me a young mare, of a fine breed: she gave five colts, which my father purposed should be given to my brothers; after that she gave three more, making altogether eight colts. I returned to my mistress, and gave an account of what I found. At the end of five or six days, I asked her if she had examined the bills; she answered calmly, "not yet"; and I went to inform the Creole, Rosa Brindiz, who had the care of my sister, Maria del Rosario. Rosa was continually urging me not to lose any opportunity of asking my mistress about it, as she wanted my sister's share, to repay herself the expenses of nursing and keeping her, and as I was the eldest, it was my duty, she said, to look after the money. Teased by her, I ventured to mention it again to my mistress; but what was my astonishment, when instead of money, she said, "You are in a great hurry for your inheritance, do you not know that I am the lawful heir of my slaves? if you speak to me again about it, I will send you where you will never see the sun nor the moon again; go and clean the furniture." The following day I made Rosa acquainted with this answer, and some days after she came herself to speak to my mistress, with whom she was a long time; when she came out I gave her two of the three bracelets, and all the beads. My mistress, who was always watching me, came near us, and intimated to Rosa, that she disliked her to have any communication with me, or any of the servants, and Rosa went away, and never came there any more.

As for me, from the moment that I lost my hopes, I ceased to be a faithful slave; from an humble, submissive being, I turned the most discontented of mankind: I wished to have wings to fly from that place, and to go to Havana; and from that day my only thoughts were in planning how to escape and run away. Some days after I sold to a silver-smith the other bracelet, and for which he gave me seven dollars, and some reals; I gave the dollars to a priest, for prayers to be said for my poor mother. It was not long before my mistress knew of it, through the priest; she asked me where I had the money from, I told her; she wanted to know the name of the silver-smith, I said I did not know; she flew into a passion, "You will know then for what you are born, you cannot dispose of any thing without my consent." She then sent me to the Molino for the third time. Don Saturnino, the mayoral, inquired what had I done, I told him, very peevishly, and weeping, for I did not care for the consequences at that moment, but he pitied me, untied my arms, and sent me to his kitchen, with orders not to stir from there. At the end of ten days, he said to me, "As your mistress is coming tomorrow to breakfast here, to save appearances, I will put on you the fetters, and send you to work; but if she inquires whether you have been whipped, you must say, yes." Next morning, about nine, she sent for me, gave me a new suit of clothes; and when I went to him to deliver the coarse ones, with an angry tone, he said to me, "Now, mind what you are about; in less than two months you have been sent to me three times, and I have treated you kindly, endeavour to do your best not to come here again, if you do, you shall be treated severely; go to your mistress, go, and beware." I went to my mistress, and threw myself at her feet, she bade me get up, and ordered a good breakfast for me; but I could not eat anything, my heart was uneasy; Havana, with all the happy days I enjoyed there, was continually in my mind, and my only wish was to go there. My mistress observed with wonder my not eating breakfast, particularly of some nice stew she ordered for me: the truth is, that she could not do without me for a length of time, and this was the reason that my journeys to the Molino never exceeded nine or ten days; and although she struck me so often, and degraded me, calling me always the worst of all the Creoles born in the Molino, I was still attached to her, and shall never forget the care she had taken on my education.

After this she treated me with more kindness; she allowed me to go fishing, which was my most pleasant amusement. Next morning my mistress went to the house of the Senora Gomez, where they played at cards, and it was my duty to stand behind her chair all the time; if she was a winner I carried home the money bag, and when I delivered it to her she put her hand into it and gave me some. She was much pleased, when she saw me making myself a pair of trousers, which I learned myself; for since the idea of freedom took possession of my mind, I endeavoured to learn every thing useful to me; I invented many fancy things in my leisure hours, though these were few, I took sheets of paper, and doubling them in different shapes and forms, I turned them in various shapes as flowers, pine-apples, shells, fans, epaulettes, and many more things, for which I was praised by everybody. As my mistress treated me with a little more kindness, I insensibly began to be more calm, my heart more composed, and to forget her late harsh behaviour towards me. I began to be as comfortable as ever; in a word, I thought myself already free, and waited only to be of age; this hope encouraged me to learn many useful things, so that if I should not be a slave I should earn a honest livelihood. At this time I wrote a great many sonnets. Poetry requires an object, but I had none to enflame my breast, this was the cause of my verses being nothing else than poor imitations. I was very anxious to read every book or paper that fell in my way, either at home or in the streets, and if I met with any poetry I learnt it by heart, in consequence of this, I could recite many things in poetry. Besides, when my mistress had company at dinner, and that was almost every day, she had always some poet invited who recited verses and composed sonnets extempore; I had in a corner of the room some ink in an egg-shell and a pen, and while the company applauded and filled their glasses with wine away I went to my corner, and wrote as many verses as I could remember.

Three or four months after this, as my mistress was unwell, she was advised to go to the bathing town of Madruga to bathe; with her complaint she turned cross and peevish; she reproached my having disposed of my mother's trinkets, having five brothers, and that that was a robbery, and that if I was put in possession of the inheritance, I soon would lose it in gambling, and she was continually threatening me with the Molino and with Don Saturnino, whose last words were imprinted on my heart, and I had no wish to pay him another visit. With the belief that if I could go to Havana I would have my liberty, I inquired the distance, and was told twelve leagues, which I could not reach on foot in one night; I then dropt for the present that idea, waiting for a better opportunity. It was my custom to clean myself and change twice a week, and one day before dressing I went to bathe in a bath, thirty yards distant; while in the bath my mistress called me, in an instant I dressed myself and was before her, "What were you doing in the bath? Who gave you liberty to go? Why did you go?" were her angry inquiries, and with her fist she made my nostrils bleed profusely; all this happened at the street-door, and before all the people, but what confused me more was, that there lived opposite a young mulatto girl, of my own age, the first who inspired me with love, a thing I did not feel before; or rather I loved her as a sister, and our intercourse was kept up by some little presents from one to another, and I told her that I was free. About ten o'clock, my mistress ordered my shoes to be taken off and my head shaved, after which I was commanded to carry water for the use of the house, with a large barrel upon my head; the brook was distant thirty yards with a declivity towards it from the side of the house; I went, filled the barrel, and with some help I put it upon my head, I was returning up the little hill, when my foot missed, and down I went upon my knee, the barrel falling a little forward came rolling down, struck against my chest, and down both tumbled in the brook. My mistress said, "that is a trick of your's to evade work," she threatened me with the Molino and Don Saturnino, which name had a magic effect on me, and I began to think seriously about escaping to Havana. The following morning when all the people were at church, a free servant called me aside, and in a whisper, said to me, "my friend, if you suffer it is your fault; you are treated worse than the meanest slave; make your escape, and present yourself before the Captain-General at Havana, state your ill treatment to him, and he will do you justice"; at the same time showing me the road to Havana.

At eleven o'clock, I saw Don Saturnino arrive at the house; from this moment my heart beat violently, my blood was agitated, and I could not rest, I trembled like a leaf, my only comfort at that moment was the solitude of my room, there I went; and there I heard the servants talking together, one was inquiring of the other the reason of the coming of Don Saturnino. "Why," said the other, "to take away Juan F." This was more than I could endure, a general trembling took possession of my limbs, and my head ached very much. I fancied myself already in the hands of Don Saturnino, leading me away tied like the greatest criminal—from this moment I determined on my escape. I left my room with this determination, when I met again the same servant, who said to me, "Man take out that horse from the stable, and leave him outside, for fear that when Don Saturnino may want him in the night, you will make too much noise, and will disturb your mistress—here are the spurs, take them, and there is the saddle, and so you will know where to find every thing." And then he gave me such a look as quite convinced me that, he advised me to take the opportunity, and not lose it. I was hesitating, yet I did not like to leave behind me my brothers, and then I was afraid to travel a whole night through roads unknown to me, and alone, and in danger of falling in with any commissary of police; but what was my surprise, when after supper, as I was sitting on a bench by myself, meditating about what to do, Don Saturnino came to me, and asked, "Where do you sleep?" I pointed to him the place and he went away; this entirely determined me to make my escape—he might have made the inquiry with a good intention, but I could not consider it but with great suspicion. I remembered at that moment the fate of one of my uncles, who in a case like mine, took the same determination of escaping to Havana, to Don Nicolas, Don Manuel, and the Senor Marques and was brought back again like a wild beast—but for all that I resolved to venture on my escape, and in case of detection, to suffer for something. I waited till twelve o'clock. That night everybody retired early, it being very cold and rainy. I saddled the horse for the first time in my life, put on the bridle, but with such trembling that I hardly knew what I was about, after that I knelt down, said a prayer, and mounted the horse. When I was going away, I heard the sound of a voice saying, "God bless you, make haste." I thought that nobody saw me, but as I knew afterwards, I was seen by several of the negroes, but nobody offered any impediment to my flight. Juan——.

—1840